"As Drs. Schmitt and Cooter have addressed the problem that few doctors have been able to find a solution for...the aldehyde poisoning caused by *Candida albicans,* they are to be commended. Dr. Cooter says ... 'If you have adequate amounts of glutamine, selenium, niacin, folic acid, B6, B12, iron and molybdenum, aldehydes continue to be metabolized into acetic acid, which can be excreted, or converted further into acetyl coenzyme A ...a necessary part of the Krebs energy cycle necessary for the health and maintenance of all cells.".... A candida treatment was also formulated under Dr. Cooter's name, called Exspore™. We believe the findings of Stephan Cooter are well worth investigating for yourselves."

—Anthony Di Fabio, from the supplement to *The Art of Getting Well,* **The Rheumatoid Disease Foundation**

"...impressively thorough..."

—Terrence Young, M.D., D.C., Acupuncturist

"Chronic Illness has one big pattern with many small differences. Some of the causes can be traced to diet...contaminated meat...white rice, white flour, sugar...toxic chemical exposure, history of vaccines...opportunistic microbes that begin to cause damage when the system has been weakened. Chronic Illness is a deficiency disease, worsened by childhood illness, vaccination, and many other toxic agents."

—*Beating Chronic Illness*

"Dr. Stephan Cooter is totally refreshing to read. He's always on the leading edge of research, constantly experimenting, making new discoveries that make you think about and see alternative health information in new and exciting ways. He clearly integrates and focuses information that's practical. What he writes about, I can use. He's exciting to be around in person. It's a pleasure to work with him."

—Carol Cooper, D.C., Nutritional Counselor, Chair of the Health Empowerment Coalition

"Molybdenum sufficiency may be a chief player in transforming metabolic toxins in our bodies into sources of restful sleep and vitality at the same time it reduces the waistline. Rather than strangle in our own environmental and cellular waste, humble nutrients may help us recycle our garbage and turn it into energy for our cells."

—*Beating Chronic Illness*

"It's not merely the knowledge and intelligence that shine through his work, but his vision. He's one of only two healers who've ever done anything for me. He's a genius."

—Sandra Loy, author of *The Writer's Voice*, Holt & Rheinhart

"I suspect there is a real chemistry of love, a real chemistry of joy and vitality, and that it would be registered in the system as health...Our language is a metaphor of what our bodies are telling us ...we can reeducate the neurons by what we say to ourselves."

—*Beating Chronic Illness*

"...completely readable. I loved the term Acquired Immune Sufficiency...The way Stephan Cooter uses psychosomatic to refer to health is also well thought of in alternative health circles, by both physicians and metaphysicians alike."

—Guruka Khalsa, D.C.

"Our immune systems were programmed to destroy the body or the mind of the person who didn't fit in... To learn from a Wall Street Economist, 'The majority is always wrong.'"

—*Beating Chronic Illness*

"*Beating Chronic Illness* is truth and science with a heart beat. Dr. Stephan Cooter is an excellent researcher and thinker."

—John Mock, M.A., Educator and Consultant, Somatic Processes

"...one of the purposes...served by illness is to learn how to get along, how to get along with our human environment, our emotions, and our microbes."

——*Beating Chronic Illness*

Beating Chronic Illness

By

Stephan Cooter, Ph.D.

ProMotion Publishing

San Diego, California

Beating Chronic Illness

Published by:

ProMotion Publishing
10387 Friars Road
Suite 231
San Diego, CA 92120
1 (800) 231-1776

© Stephan Cooter

ISBN 0-9636328-6-8

Foreword

When compared to the world's population, there are a tiny almost insignificant percentage who actually pierce the veil of authoritarianism of which there are two kinds.

One kind is spelled with a capital "A," as in "Authority." Authority relies on our blind belief that the Authority figure knows what is best for us. We do all their bidding blindly because they all have our best interests at heart.

A slave has the same advantage, with such a kindly master!

But sometimes these powerful people are right, and it is to our best interests to blindly follow a set of rules that they have laid down and which we have accepted on faith.

Unfortunately, an Authority of this kind is also most often wrong and does not know why the rules have been laid down or why they should be followed. If A happens, then does B, each and every time. That B should inevitably and always follow behind A is also a good description of a stimulus-response mechanism—and insanity.

The other kind of "authority" begins with a small "a." This kind describes an erudite person who is knowledgeable in a particular discipline, such that we know that we can rely on his/her wisdom and act accordingly.

Unfortunately, in the field of the practice of medicine, the vast majority of physicians—licensed "healers"—are of the first kind, "Authorities spelled with a capital A. They do not know why they prescribe a certain treatment modality or what are its results. They prescribe "standard care" because they've been taught to do so; because their peers will frown on them if they do not; because insurance will not pay their fee, otherwise; because they may lose their license if they are to deviate in the patient's interest.

As a general rule, a human disease condition, therefore, is treated by stimulus-response modalities by Authorities, not by authorities—and this is insanity!

The small fraction of the human population who understand the relationship between Authority and authority, like the author, Stephan Cooter, Ph.D., of *Beating Chronic Illness*, have found a satisfying life-goal consisting generally of two parts. They have first the joy and deep satisfaction of taking responsibility for increasing spheres of activities in their own life, for abiding wellness comes only through personal knowledge and self-application. It is only one's body that produces wellness, not Authority. They have additional pleasure of sharing their findings with others who are also afflicted and face seemingly insurmountable odds. The man who first glimmers the lighthouse and safe harbor beyond the shoals would be evil indeed, who did not also inform others.

Stephan Cooter, Ph.D., has suffered more than a life-time of agony and bad Authoritarian advice. At last, however, he was able to pierce the veil, to take responsibility for his own wellness. In so doing, he has also become an authority—spelled with a small "a," an erudite and knowledgeable individual. His *Beating Chronic Illness*, while admittedly speculative in wide-ranging hypothesis, is also concrete. Those suffering from Post Polio Syndrome, Fibromyalgia, Chronic Fatigue Syndrome, MS, and many other chronic diseases will want to know of Cooter's personal path, hopefully to save time and pain in their own search for wellness.

Victims of Rheumatoid Arthritis, and the more than 75 other collagen tissue diseases which the The Arthritis Fund now calls "Rheumatoid Diseases" will also find important data for their own personal search toward wellness. Candidiasis, for example, is a concomitant of the Rheumatoid Disease condition virtually 100% of the time, just as also it seems to be for Post Polio Syndrome, Fibromyalgia, Lupus, and Chronic Fatigue Syndrome. The narration on how Dr. Cooter was able to first perceive the problem, and then to solve it, is must reading for all of those suffering a chronic condition.

On behalf of the Arthritis Fund, I personally recommend that *Beating Chronic Illness* be absorbed for all its narration on false starts and eventual successes.

Join the small but growing percentage of us who have begun to define our own health-path, and who are each of us becoming erudite, knowledgeable authorities—spelled with a small "a."

Cordially,

Perry A. Chapdelaine, Sr.,
Executive Director
The Arthritis Fund
5106 Old Harding Road
Franklin, TN 37064

Dedication

I dedicate this book to Mrs. Dorothy Haskins of Denver who said that I should write this book because it would change the way people think and feel about themselves and that it would become part of a mega-trend in making patients and physicians alike more informed about natural sources of healing. "You have healing in your hands," Mrs. Haskins said, "and you extend healing to whomever you touch." Well, I am not a physician although I had made it my life-long responsibility to be as informed as possible about health and disease. When no one knew the solution to my problems, I was forced to seek the answers myself. I think this may be typical of people who suffer. When you have life questions, you seek life answers. Without a life problem, no one seeks to find a solution.

I am also a member of the Health Empowerment Coalition. It has a mission statement that reads as follows: "To raise public awareness of the availability, viability and efficacy of natural health approaches. To help people overcome the fear of thinking for themselves by promoting the empowering belief that the individual's intuition and observations have as much importance in the healing process as the wellness professional's knowledge and skills."

I have so empowered myself by default. No one could tell me what I needed to know.

Occasionally, I am smart enough to see a metaphor where one was intended. When Mrs. Haskins said that I had healing in my hands, I came to know that it was a metaphorical statement. I write with my hands. My hope is that you will make it your responsibility as a person, patient, and physician to become informed about health; and, if you are a physician, to begin to read outside of your primary field: the findings of original scientific research in related fields, orthodox and unorthodox therapies that apply directly to your field, not just American journals but European, Russian, Chinese, and Japanese studies, to name a few. The world is rich in medical information, but America has only in a few instances been willing to import it. America is a Third World in poverty of information about health. What is more, it is my hope that physicians learn to honor what patients know about their own health and disease.

I believe too that the large pharmaceutical companies could do both themselves and ourselves a favor by following the same line of thinking. It is rumored that they have been picking on the small growth companies by exerting little pressures here and there that discourage research, discourage publication of research results, and erect little Iron Curtains of trade protectionism. It would seem to make common sense to think differently. If other world pharmaceutical companies like the 80 companies in Japan which are producing Coenzyme Q10 have a good thing going, and let me tell you they do, then why not join them. Why fight a good thing. The more who cooperate, the more we will know, the more competition, the better off our health and prices we pay to get it. For instance, it is a commonplace observation that Q10 when added to any drug therapy does two things: the therapeutic end is reached and side effects either do not exist or are minimal. What could be better? You get to market your old product, you get to research and sell a new one, and you get to have the real satisfaction that your product has helped people get well.

May the spirit that guided my hands in writing this guide yours in discovering the road to your own good health and the road to promoting it in others. Many chronic illnessness have been and can be beaten. A little thought to better nutrition, better digestion and assimilation of nutrients, better elimination of your own metabolic wastes, other toxins, and the wastes of the microbes you harbor may amply repay all of your efforts.

Acknowledgments

I want to thank Richard T. Hall, M.D., former head of March of Dimes in Riverside, California, for making me wait in his office two hours beyond the time of my appointment. As I waited, I began to understand something about attitudes in the medical profession. I became angry for one thing, angry at how I was treated, angry that I was not given any dignity as a patient or a person. I have been angry now 34 years. I want to thank Dr. Hall because that anger helped motivate me to find answers that he could not provide me with. I also want to thank Donald Roberts, M.D., specializing in internal medicine, for a similar reason. When he couldn't find an answer to my chronic fatigue, my depression, my insomnia, and my overall weakness, he sent me to a psychiatrist for psychosomatic illness. That too made me angry. That anger helped sustain me for twenty years. It was fuel to live on, and as I thought about it, it helped me figure out, Dr. Roberts, that there is also something called psychosomatic health.

It occurred to me that much of our society in teaching, in parenting, in churching, in politics, in our relationships with friends, in our relationship with spouses, does very little towards promoting the attitudes of wellness. One of those attitudes is thinking the best of another person. Some call this a spiritual attitude or a religious attitude. And I believe it is just that. But for the benefit of those who specialize, I'd like to be one of the first who points out that thinking the best of the other person is not just a good sermon, it is also a way of living, of treating one's spouse, both children and parents, friends, both students and teachers, both doctor AND patient. It is a way of living and it is a new ethical base for how doctors think of patients, but it is an old base of how patients have normally thought of doctors. I will exclude myself from that norm with some exceptions.

One of those exceptions is Guruka Khalsa, D.C. I'd like to thank Dr. Guruka Khalsa for many things. She, on the contrary, encouraged me to believe that I could in fact and in truth find the way to my own health if I just looked. She was generous enough to loan me much of her well-stocked medical library and to discuss the observations and intuitions I came up with. She was also generous enough to read and comment on my manuscript.

I'd like to thank Margorie Eng, Acupuncturist, for repeatedly telling me that my tongue said I was experiencing digestive upset. She is the kind of old fashioned health professional who can diagnose you from your tongue. As I repeatedly denied that what she said was a true reading of my condition, it too helped me to discover the main cause of what is called the Post Polio Syndrome, Chronic Fatigue Syndrome, and many other chronic conditions of illness. Presently, there is a whole line of research mentioned in G.I.N.I.'s *International Polio Network* newsletter that has observed that

Post Polio Syndrome people commonly, if not universally, experience "digestive upset." The Texas study identifies the upset as stomach bloating, gas, constipation-diarrhea, hemorrhoid syndrome, exactly what I had. I believe you'll be interested in what I found. I know the cause. And the implications of resolving the causes of infection and the toxins involved apply to beating chronic illness involving fatigue, pain, insomnia, weakness and foggy thinking. Post Polio Syndrome, Lupus, Multiple Sclerosis, Parkinson's, and Alzheimer's share many of the symptoms of chronic illness: knowing about fungal and viral infections, slow infection or autoimmune psuedoinfection, exposure to antibiotics and vaccines, malnutrition, toxic accumulations, and mal-elimination may all play roles in resolving these chronic problems. Lifestyle, thinking well of yourself, detoxification, good nutrition and supplementation may all play important roles in what you can do to get well.

And for Carol Cooper, D.C., I want to thank you for participating in my karma or the fateful chance encounters of things, the magical synchronicity of providing me with the last piece of the puzzle I needed to pick up, and the fateful appearance of a nutrient salesperson who left behind a fateful bottle of molybdenum from Nutri-West and a fateful article written by Wally Schmitt. All played an important role in putting my health and work together. In relation to Dr. Schmitt, I believe he is capable of giving ideas and advice to many research institutes, many industrial companies, and pointing their heads in the directions that they would never have considered taking, but roads which may lead to a very different and vibrant 21st century.

And I want to thank Allen Taylor for many reasons. He had many magical effects on me. For one, he is a natural interviewer or health counselor, or wise person. In his presence and with his encouragement, I was able to talk out, see, and discover a wealth of connections that led to many health discoveries, and many more fascinating, unanswered questions that only clinical research, scientific research, self-help groups, self-empowered groups, the health food industry, the food industry, and the pharmaceutical industries will be able to answer. He helped create for me a new paradigm, one that is both cooperative and kind, benevolent and good. Imagine a world where all the health resources in all nations cooperate, where patients have dignity, where patients empower themselves to overcome the fear of thinking for themselves and where doctors overcome the prejudice that their patients' observations and insights don't matter, where scientist and doctor together work in one place, working to find answers to health and curing disease. Imagine for the moment every football and basketball fan having the same access to all the phases of health care that football and basketball players have. Imagine doctors taking notes on what patients say and handing their questions to the army of scientists s/he employs in his or her office because the patient is honored and the patient's observations are considered sacred. Imagine the scientists using informed patients as consultants. Imagine the FDA balancing their Advisory Panels with all levels of industry and health care and patients and consumers of ALL interest groups and individuals. Imagine a homeopath on an FDA Advisory Panel with all the dignity that homeopathy enjoys in Britain. Imagine chiropractors both orthodox and unorthodox on those Advisory Panels. Imagine naturopaths, acupuncturists, and health food stores from not only the U.S. but from Europe, the new Russia, and other former Soviet Union countries, all Arabic countries, all South American Countries, Canada, everywhere balancing such committees not only in the United States but in all countries. The AMA and FDA need the traditional medicine attitudes of the Muslim, the Chinese, and the Native American. For traditional medicine people, the patient and the cure are considered a living spirit. They forbid the use of dissection and cadavers for one basic reason: concentration on death ignores the living spirit of health. The FDA and AMA need to rub elbows and souls with the idea that health is the product of living balance to help it return to its original mission of 1906, its 1962 mission that food additives and synthetic drugs must be proved safe and effective before they go into common use. At the very least, warning labels about food additives should be written on all labels of medicines and all foods that list BOTH pro and con allegations. Imagine seeing a sign that says this food is irradiated: irradiation is said to be good for extending its shelf life but may be hazardous to its nutritional content. Imagine buying a prescription drug that listed the side effects and the hazards of long term and short term use as well as its alleged benefits. Imagine that such labeling honors the dignity not only of the company's positive research but of the consumer-patients' right to know. Imagine the employment opportunities that this will create. Imagine the wealth of information that would be aired in a simple committee meeting. Imagine the billions of ideas that would be generated for research nearly every day. Imagine employing the unemployed in some of these tasks.

Imagine a world of cooperation and mutuality.

Imagine a world of balanced dignity for supplier and consumer alike.

Now imagine how things are.

It is hard to imagine.

Introduction

You May Have A Time Bomb Ticking Inside

How are you feeling lately? Do you think you're growing old, and that's why you don't have the strength and energy you used to have? One over-the-counter enzyme may reverse all that. For others, it's one missing amino acid.

You thought you had a touch of the flu, but somehow you can't quite kick it, and get back in gear. One amino acid and one mineral may change that. You think you work too hard and that's why you can't get to sleep or stay asleep at night. Have you thought of taking your vitamins at night, rather than in the morning? One vitamin can make you sleepy, and it can be used to your advantage at night.

You simply ignore the pains you've been getting, you're a little depressed but that's natural, but you've begun to forget things more easily and it bothers you. Where did you put your glasses this time?

If any of these descriptions are true, this book has your name written all over it.

Six months after finishing *Beating Chronic Illness*, I learned of the work of Tedd Koren and Michael Culbert. In it, I found a fascinating confirmation of my theory that anyone who has been vaccinated may be subject to many of the conditions I was diagnosed with, including slow Pertussis infection, Post Polio Syndrome, Chronic Fatigue, Mononucleosis, autoimmune disorders, allergies, immune system weakness, and Lupus. It should have been obvious many years ago from the known "adverse reactions" to vaccinations. And it should have been listed under Poliomyelitis in the 1992 *Merck Manual*. Instead, you will find it under two other headings: Aseptic Meningitis, known causes, and under the discussion of Vitamin B1 deficiency known as beriberi. Beriberi is caused not only by the eating of white rice, but sugar and white bread.

Michael Culbert, D.Sc., Bradford Research Institute, 1993, reported that their clinical team began seeing scattered cases of Post Polio Syndrome in adults in the 1980s. Post Polio Syndrome (PPS) is a condition very closely resembling Chronic Fatigue Syndrome (CFS), Fibromyalgia syndrome (FM), Lupus, and Multiple Sclerosis (MS): all of these chronic illnesses show symptoms of muscular weakness, muscular and neural pain, insomnia, sleep disturbances, and problems with thinking. Post Polio Syndrome has been commonly diagnosed only in people who had originally experienced an acute polio infection 20 to 30 years before, however. So the Bradford doctors could have just as easily identified the condition as CFS, FM, or beriberi.

What was surprising to the Bradford doctors was that these cases of what they had diagnosed as PPS were in people who had NOT had polio. The patients they found PPS in had only had polio vaccines.

To Dr. Culbert, it was "one more piece of evidence that vaccines alone may constitute a possible contributory factor to CFS and other syndromes, including AIDS." All of these syndromes involve immune system weakness, slow infection, and a host of common symptoms.

AIDS? Some research in 1992 linked the origin of AIDS directly with early vaccine production because the kidney cells of African green monkeys used to culture polio vaccine in the 1950s were infected with a Simian version of the AIDS virus. If Dr. Richard Murray is correct, many viruses and bacteria, as many as 5,000 other microbes live in vaccines. And the various agents used to sterilize the vaccines and prevent these 5,000 bugs from becoming a problem may themselves create other problems: formalin or formaldehyde is used to weaken viruses in manufacturing vaccines; various antibiotics are used to sterilize the vaccine medium; and mercury compounds are used to prevent further contamination. All three of these weakening and sterilizing agents are known causes of nerve disorders, even death by anaphylactic shock. Antibiotics and mercury themselves are known causes of pathogenic bacteria mutating into new and virulent strains.

Japanese research found the same species of monkeys used for polio vaccines to be infected with HHV-6, one of the usual viruses found in AIDS patients. Those who earlier thought that a monkey virus had jumped species would be gratified to know that the virus didn't have to jump farther than a Petri dish or a biochemist's culturing medium.

Peter Duesberg, a microbiologist, now joined by a growing number of similar voices, does not believe that any of the viruses associated with AIDS are the cause of AIDS. His reasoning is elegant: not all of the people with AIDS have a single virus, or a group of viruses in common.

What they all have in common is vaccination or prior histories of many injections. It may not be the street needle at all. Medical injections themselves may be the chief cause of polio, AIDS, MS, SIDS, cancer, leukemia, lupus, and other autoimmune disorders. The 1980 Physicians' *Desk Reference* innocently notes that vaccines have an immunosuppressing effect, "laying the foundation for the appearance of autoimmune diseases." To make this a widespread public concern would seriously impair the merchandising of a $135 million industry, not to mention many medical services.

In 1954, a quietly ignored *Lancet* article pointed out that polio epidemics began after inoculation programs. There were serious epidemics in the years 1936, 1937, 1941, 1944, 1946, 1949, and 1954. Factors that were found to provoke or increase the severity of polio were: vaccination itself, trauma, tonsillectomies, pertussis vaccines, and many injections including penicillin. In one case, an epidemic of polio broke out two weeks after a small pox vaccination campaign in Los Angeles, 1949. Similar vaccination campaigns were associated with the origin of AIDS in Haiti and Africa. A major polio epidemic took place in Israel after mass vaccinations in 1958.

In a 1983 UCLA School of Medicine and LA County Health Department study of 145 SIDS victims, 53 had been given DPT immunizations just before their deaths: 27 people died within 28 days following immunization, 17 within a week, and 6 within 24 hours. How many diseases of middle age could be traced back to problems that may have ticked away for 10 to 30 years before from similar vaccinations?

A British study considered the risk factor from vaccines remote since it found only 1 in 110,000 shots resulted in immediate neurological reactions, and permanent brain damage only occurred in 1 in 310,000 shots. This is hardly reassuring since the British vaccines were less potent, and high-risk children were excluded from the study. High-risk individuals in the United States are not excluded, nor are high-risk children excluded in Third World Countries. In WHO, *Weekly Epidemiology Record*, 1981, 56:-131-32, it was noted that India has been subject to 70,000 new cases of polio per year. These epidemics took place after community health services were in place, not before (*Lancet*, August 13, 1988, Lapil Sood). Although Dr. Sood believed that epidemics must have been greater before vaccination programs, it apparently escaped his attention that epidemics, in actual fact, took place AFTER community health vaccination programs.

Other studies suggest that 1 in 875 DPT shots produce immediate convulsions, shock, brain inflammation or death. No studies exist to correlate the incidence of Motor Neuron Disease, (FM, CFS, PPS, MS, AMS) with vaccination from months to years before. However, about 20% of India's population develops Motor Neuron Disease, exactly the same percentage as develops in the rest of the world (M. Gourie Devi, and others, "Pattern of motor neuron disease in South India and monomelic amyotrophy,' in *Motor Neurone Disease*, New Delhi, 1987: 217-228). If so, it is not only 20% of people who were diagnosed with acute polio infections who are at risk, or 500,000 in the US, but untold millions of people world wide.

Contrary to the official stance of those who believe in vaccinations, the uncelebrated failure of the 135-million-dollar US vaccination industry shows a general 400% increase in diseases that have been vaccinated against since the 1950's, according to the *Townsend Letter for Doctors*, October, 1992. Where polio vaccination programs have been instituted worldwide, reported paralytic polio infections show a 700% increase as a result of compulsory vaccination. In fact, all officially recorded cases of polio since 1979 are said to be caused by vaccination itself.

There is one exception, not usually mentioned. *Morbidity and Mortality Weekly*, (1992) reported an outbreak of wild polio virus infection in the

Netherlands, apparently 54 cases. The incident was used to encourage or scare people into making sure their vaccinations were up to date before they travel. Had it not been a religious group which refused to accept vaccination, the "outbreak" would have been reported as "aseptic spinal meningitis." If you object to polio vaccination, and you get "polio"; it is usually called "polio" after 1954. If you've been vaccinated, and you get "polio," it is called "meningitis." Polio has not been wiped out. Epidemics were eradicated by changing the way the disease was reported, according to Tedd Koren, D.C.

In *Polio Network News*, Winter 1992, it was reported that 4,236 petitions have been filed with the U.S. Claims Court for injuries and deaths caused by polio vaccinations. Of these claims, only 611 have been processed; and of those processed, 230 have been awarded compensation of $48,000 to $2.9 million. Out of 2,478 claims examined by the federal Department of Health and Human Services, about half of the claims, 1,719 claims, concerned death and injury following DPT/Polio vaccination. Of the 230 awards granted by the court, 51 of the awards were for deaths caused by vaccination. Forty-two of 51 deaths were ruled to be misclassified as sudden infant death syndrome (SIDS). The court has ruled the government is liable for injuries caused over several decades of polio vaccine.

You won't read about that in the major media. You get glimpses of it only in such publications as the Winter 1993, *Polio Network News*. There, it is a curiosity. Elsewhere it is not something worth reporting on.

The World Health Organization claims that 80% of the world's children have been vaccinated against common childhood diseases and that this has resulted in preventing the deaths of 3.2 million children. I hope this is true. But at best, the prevention is temporary, and the risks are enormous. 400% to 700% increases in childhood illnesses may be caused by vaccination itself, not by failing to vaccinate.

The Clinton Administration is interested in promoting more aggressive vaccination programs. In view of the problems created by vaccination, greater attempts to vaccinate have ironic implications for the consumer. Vaccination programs should be rethought by all of us. All the data sitting unexamined in the Department of Health and Human Services must not have reached the Secretary's of HHS's attention, either that or the presidential vaccination-company lobbies may be very entertaining.

Tedd Koren, D.C., quoted Barbara Fisher, who served 10 years on the National Vaccine Advisory Committee trying to reform the health care system herself, as revealing more than presidential election lobby monies: "We have bad science and bad medicine translated into law to ensure that vaccine manufacturers make big profits, that career bureaucrats at the Public Health Service meet the mass vaccination goals promised to politicians funding their budgets, and pediatricians have a steady flow of patients...As the drug companies have often stated in meetings I have attended, if a vaccine they produce is not mandated to be used on a mass basis, they do not recoup their R & D costs and don't make the profit they want...official studies of vaccine risk have been designed and conducted by physicians who sit on vaccine policy-making committees at the Centers for Disease Control...some of whom receive money from vaccine manufacturers for their universities and for testifying as expert witnesses in vaccine-injury cases. And others are federal employees with an eye on career advancement within HHS and a future job with a vaccine manufacturer after retirement from public service" (*Well Mind Association*, October 1993).

Many forces may work against the public being well informed about vaccination. When one PPS survivor, Ted Kutzer, asked me if I got my flu shots this year, I said, "No, I don't want to take the risk."

Ted said, "You're a high risk individual, you know."

I pointed to the information table where my article, "Say No to Vaccines," was resting. I said, "I know, I'm high risk. That's why I'm not getting any shots anymore."

Beriberi or Aseptic Spinal Meningitis?

Getting shots is only one player in producing what I believe are the true causes behind Chronic Illness. There are many.

Under THIAMINE (VITAMIN B-1) DEFICIENCY, T*he Merck Manual* (1992), you will find that B1 deficiency is commonly caused by dextrose and alcohol as well as eating white rice. You will also find that Harvey Wiley, MD, in *The History of a Crime Against the Food Law* (1929), warned the food industry against using dextrose, or corn sugar, in any of its forms as a sweetener and preservative in processed food because he found that it encouraged generalized "debility" in the young men who ate canned food with dextrose used as sugar.

In digestion, any refined sugar can be converted into alcohol, then acetaldehyde, by the GI tract's intestinal flora. Although Dr. Wiley didn't know that mechanism, the *Merck Manual*'s description of vitamin B1 pathology should give everyone cause to worry:

"The most advanced neural changes occur in the peripheral nerves, particularly of the legs. The distal segments are characteristically affected earliest and most severely. Degeneration of the medullary sheath has been demonstrated in all tracts of the cord, especially in the anterior horn and posterior ganglion cells. Lesions of hemorrhagic polioencephalitis occur in the brain when deficiency is severe" (page 969).

This is also a precise description of an acute polio virus infection, and yet it is a description of B1 vitamin deficiency caused damage. Why hasn't anyone noticed this strange coincidence?

As you will read, Dr. Richard Bruno, Ph.D., found brain lesions in the hypothalamus of people who had had polio diagnosed and who died in the 1950s. He believed, and he still believes, that polio virus caused the lesions, and that they were worsened by overwork and emotional stress as diagnosed polio survivors aged.

However, the most obvious cause of known brain lesions is not a virus at all, but a sugar-alcohol induced B1 vitamin deficiency that used to be known as beriberi. Here the *Merck Manual* identifies the ominous consequence of people who may not have been damaged by a virus at all, but by an industrialized diet leading to B1 deficiency. The normal industrialized diet of white bread, white rice, and sugar may be the major player in setting up early signs of beriberi characterized by "fatigue, irritation, poor memory, sleep disturbances, ... pain, anorexia, abdominal discomfort, and constipation (a *Merck* beriberi description)" that have been incorrectly associated with a virus infection.

All of these chronic fatigue symptoms are the usual symptoms of chronic illness: FM, PPS, MS, CFS, not to mention alcoholism, cerebral beriberi, Creutzfeldt-Jakob, Kuru, and Wernicke-Korsakoff syndrome. Full blown dry beriberi involves not only burning feet, gum problems, calf pains, leg pains, but extreme weakness of the legs that may extend to other parts of the body. In wet beriberi, heart problems arise leading to heart failure. Why hasn't anyone noticed that heart disease and neurological problems are related?

All of this is brought on by a demineralized, devitaminized diet, and may have been the basic dietary cause that led to acute paralysis and even death in many people diagnosed with acute polio infection. In fact, the virus may have been attracted by sites of pre-existing injury in the brain and spinal cord. Polio viral infection, I believe is a secondary cause of nerve damage, not a primary cause.

But there are many causes. As I wrote *Beating Chronic Illness*, I was convinced that childhood illnesses and vaccines played another major role. Under *Merck*'s "Poliomyelitis," you will not find any confirmation of that theory. But if you discovered as Tedd Koren, D.C., did, that polio infection was recorded only if you had a terribly acute case lasting more than two weeks after 1953, and only if you had not been vaccinated, and then, it wasn't recorded as polio at all. It was recorded as Acute Viral Encephalitis or Aseptic Meningitis, from 1953 to the present. Vaccine special interests must have had very powerful effects on the popular media and the medical sources of information.

Under meningitis headings, I found unexpected support for my theories of causes:

On page 1473, *Merck Manual*, under the heading Infectious causes, I read:

Viral causes: Mumps, echovirus, poliovirus, coxsackievirus, herpes simplex [cold sores], other herpes viruses, horse viruses, hepatitis, mononucleosis [Epstein-Barr virus, also known as a herpes virus], and, [believe it or not,] HIV.

Did you know that the AIDS virus is a causative agent in polio? Did you know that common childhood diseases are common causes of what used to be called polio?

Postinfectious causes: Measles [known to cause paralysis in sheep as well as other damage], rubella, varicella [a fancy word for chickenpox], smallpox, and cowpox.

It is not unrealistic to think there is a direct connection between childhood illnesses and vaccination and what I call chronic illness.

We might wonder why Multiple Sclerosis is listed as a non-infectious cause of meningitis formerly known as polio. They are both demyelinating conditions involving loss of the myelin sheath. They are both linked with vitamin and mineral deficiencies as you will see.

Also listed under non-infectious causes are iatrogenic causes: chemotherapeutic agents, antibiotics, dyes, lead.

Under the quiet heading vaccine reactions, you can read "MANY"[my caps], including rabies, pertussis, and smallpox. This translates: vaccines are known causes of meningitis-polio. Do you suppose your family physician has noticed this? Do you suppose anyone in the research field has noticed? I wrote one dozen international names in research to find out, but not one answered my letter.

The one *Merck* classification that makes a lot of sense is many drugs, including all over-the-counter non-narcotic painkillers, like aspirin and ibuprofen. And all we were told in the mass media is that aspirin was good for preventing heart disease and cancer. According to the 1993 Winter *FDA Consumer* report, British studies were not able to confirm the aspirin claim, and in fact found that aspirin seemed to worsen our chances of both cancer and heart disease. We might wonder how much is news report and how much on national TV is advertising that looks like news.

There are many unfortunate established causes of chronic illness, and it wouldn't hurt to know enough to help remedy the situation by eating brown rice for the natural B1 "rice polish" that cures beriberi, not synthetic B1, and all the major minerals and trace minerals we may have been deprived of most of our lives that have been missing in sugar and white bread.

Chronic Illness is a deficiency disease, worsened by childhood illnesses, vaccination, and many other toxic agents.

You Are What You Feel

And what you eat. People prone to getting "polio" and its "late effects" have been commonly identified as Type A personalities. Multiple Sclerosis patients have the Type A pattern as well. So do people with high blood pressure.

But apparently escaping the attention of researchers were the originators of the Type A observation: Drs. Meyer Friedman and Ray Rosenman invented the name, Type A behavior, to describe people predictably prone to heart disease. In accountants who did not change either their diet or exercise, when the tax deadline of April 15th approached, their entire blood chemistry changed to elevated cholesterol and every other blood serum abnormality on record. Personality, hurry, hostility, and excessive competitiveness set both humans and rats up for trouble, cardiovascular trouble.

Friedman and Roseman's rats were transformed into Type A rodents by damaging their hypothalamus. A Type A rat not only fights another Type A rat to the death, but develops heart problems in the process. As Robert Ornstein has pointed out, a Type A personality who withholds his or her hostility also becomes depressed and eventually develops cancer.

Cruetzfield-Jakob Disease, Kuru, Post Polio Syndrome, CFS, CFIDS, FM, MS, and victims of B1 beriberi deficiency may all develop a damaged hypothalamus, one with poor hormone balance, norepinephrine deficiencies, serotonin deficiencies, abnormal blood flow to the brain, sleep disturbances, weakness, memory problems, exercise intolerance, and autoimmune hyperactivity (See Vicki Carpman, "Open Your Mind to the Possibilites: L.A. Conference Explains the CFIDS Brain," *CFIDS Chronicle*, Summer 1993, for the CFS-FM commonalities). Chronic illness has one big pattern with many small differences. Some of the causes can be traced to diet, the eating of meat contaminated with Scrappie from vegetarian animals fed scraps of sheep remnants. Some of the causes can be traced to the eating of white rice, white flour, and sugar. Some of the causes can be attributed to toxic chemical exposure, and history of vaccines. Still other causes have been traced to opportunistic microbes that begin to cause damage when the system has been weakened by (1) some of these causes and/ or (2) all of these causes.

Not only knowing these causes, but using dietary remedies from food and supplements helped turned chronic illness back into health for the author, for 2/3's of the people in his study who remedied only one deficiency by taking a single trace mineral, molybdenum. There are many such simple solutions that may turn flu-like weakness back into a surplus of energy or an improved quality of life.

People with Type-A personalities hyperventilate and their rapid shallow breathing does the same thing to the pH of the blood that excess salt in the diet does: alkalosis (Richard Miller, "The Psychophysiology of Respiration," *Somatics*, 1993). An excessive alkaline pH alone can account for mineral and vitamin deficiencies. Slow abdominal-breathing is not just relaxing. It makes up for oxygen, carbon-dioxide deficiencies. Relaxing, slowing down, and simple changes in habits can help save your health.

Deficiency can be turned into sufficiency. Chronic Illness can be beaten.

Contents

Chapter 1

IN SEARCH OF
THE UNKNOWN GERM

The Syndrome of Chronic Fatigue, Pain, Weakness, Insomnia, Foggy Thinking, Depression

- How I tested positive for Mononucleosis; then, germs disappeared
- Symptoms: clumsiness, falling, lack of energy, insomnia, weakness, problems with dexterity, handwriting changes, depression, pain, memory problems
- Caution: over-exercise of weakened muscles can damage them; exercise intolerance
- Diagnosis of depression; treatment with tricyclic antidepressant
- Diagnosis of psychiatric psychosomatic illness
- Episodes of worsening and remission

If I had it to do all over again, I would be much more scientific, not for the sake of science, but for the sake of credibility. But I wasn't interested in credibility at the time, I was interested in alleviating the debilitating effects of weakness, pain, chronic fatigue, and sleeplessness. I would have traded my "good" right leg, which was no longer good, for a good night's sleep. I couldn't get to sleep and I couldn't stay that way. Most nights were passed fighting with the pillow, shooting sheep, practicing deep breathing, annoying my wife with complaints, and trying to find a position where pain didn't stab me quite as sharply. At night, I was wakeful. My days were spent sleep walking as if I were living in the haze of a dream. I was tired all the time. By the time I'd walked a block and a half to my office, I was so dead on my feet I had to lie down on the floor to begin to think about facing the work day. I'd get up from the floor, stare at the work on my desk, and wonder why my mind didn't work. I hadn't even started the day, and I had already run into the "wall," the wall of pain, fatigue, and impossibility. By the time I made it to "teach" a class, I was finished before I even started. I got students to talk for me. When I'd get up to write on the blackboard, I frequently found myself on the floor. Sometimes I taught lying down. I started falling a lot, and at first, I dismissed it as absent-minded clumsiness. I dropped things. My manual dexterity went to pot. I noticed changes in my handwriting. It was no longer recognizable. I stumbled when I walked. I ran into things. I felt dizzy sometimes, and it was hard to think or remember. I was terrified. I no longer recognized myself as me. What was happening to me?

1

I first tried an internist, who, I believed, could find anything by looking at the chemistry of blood. But he found nothing. When he asked me to perform mechanical tasks, he found a tremor in my left hand. Nerve damage, he said. Do you drink? Yes, six ounces to twelve ounces of wine with dinner. Stop drinking, he said. It's making you depressed, causing the tremor in your hand, and your overall health is terrible. Do you exercise? No, I didn't. If you don't want to drop dead, get on an exercise bike, and stay on it. I stopped drinking; I got on the bike; and I felt worse. For one thing, two drinks had dulled the pain. For another, the bike made my good right leg swell up, and the pains became intense.

I went to another doctor when I was on vacation. Mononucleosis, he said. He did a blood test and found evidence of an unknown germ: something toxic, viral, or bacterial was affecting my health. Mononucleosis is just like what you have: You're pooped all the time, aren't you? You don't even have the energy to get out of bed, do you? Nope, I didn't.

When I got back home, I went to another doctor. He couldn't find any evidence of viral activity. You're depressed, he said. And then he gave me a central nervous system stimulant, a tricyclic antidepressant. It was funny that the stimulant made me feel sleepy, but I went with it. I felt like sleeping all the time, so I did. I slept ten to twelve hours after getting the antidepressant, slept during two long naps each day, and it lasted for two weeks. Two weeks later, I felt better, and returned to work. Months later, the symptoms returned.

So I returned to the internist. Have you made the psychiatric circle yet? Nope. So on his recommendation, I went. The psychiatrist was very nervous, very quiet, and at the end of my hour gave me some little blue pills, which he said would increase norepinephrine in my brain. Take away your depression, he said. Well, both the tricyclic antidepressant and the little blue pills helped, and my pain levels were considerably improved. I didn't return to the shrink, even though it's said that psychiatrists never lose patients. They never lose them, it's said, because the problems never go away, so the patients never go away either. In my case, I thought I might be bad off, but the shrink was in worse condition than I was. So I didn't go back. Most of my life had been spent denying problems, denying that pain hurt, refusing to acknowledge that problems were not conquerable, and I resumed my normal coping mechanism. I told jokes about my problems. I flushed the little blue pills down the toilet. Humor is a survival mechanism, and laughter was my best line of defense. It still is.

But I also developed a new determination to discover what was wrong and to make it better come hell or high water. Science may advance on the shoulders of disaster, but by God, I was going to get better despite disaster. I'd look for the answers until I found them. I tried one thing after another, just as I tried one doctor after another. I was given labels: Lack of Exercise, Mononucleosis, Epstein-Barr virus which couldn't be found, clinical Depression, Psychosomatic illness, Post Polio Syndrome, Food Allergies, slow Pertussis infection, Stress, Lupus, a Candida infection that couldn't be verified. One thing was certain: I was chronically ill. Each time I was diagnosed and treated, I felt I made a small discovery, found something helpful, and it would work for a period of time, and then it would stop working. Things improved and regressed, got better, got worse. The whole nature of what is called Post Polio Syndrome or chronic illness is, by nature and by experience, episodic. I had good days, good months, bad days, bad months, finally bad years, one after another, with brief periods of remission. Then, the brief periods of remission became longer stretches of time, and they got longer, and longer, and longer still until I felt that I had found a number of things that really gave me new hope.

I had begun to apply what I had learned from decades worth of my own reading, continued experimenting, and read some more. Although I didn't quite know it at the time, I had slowly empowered myself to begin to take responsibility for my own health. I tried food supplements which helped a great deal but had made the mistake of discussing my discoveries with doctors not informed about natural approaches to health. At the time, I believed the "experts" that I was wasting my money on unnecessary food supplements, not knowing that just 5% of medical doctors had taken only one course in nutrition in their entire professional lives. So I had believed the authority of doctors rather than the authority of my own experience. Then, I began believing in what I knew and what I found. Finally, I felt I'd done it. I hadn't managed to "cure" anything, but I'd managed to find and use a number of treatments that were pretty damn good, good enough to give me long periods, months of relief from pain, months of improved strength, only occasional insomnia, and much, much less fatigue. I wanted to share what I found in the hope that it would make a difference for others with similar chronic illness. No matter what label was applied to the state of my ill health, it seemed always to amount to weakness, chronic fatigue, pain, sleeplessness, trouble with thinking. Making up nutritional deficiencies and helping remove toxic wastes from my body took care of most of them.

There are many simple strategies that work that most M.D.s are unaware of and don't recognize when they see them. When I said what I'd done, I was told that I hadn't cured any of my problems. I had only improved my general health and that was why I felt better. Well, I thought that was the point. What we all need to do is find ways to improve our general health, not treat disease.

I'm not an M.D.; I'm a professional researcher. And when my mind works, I'm a first-class thinker who can think just about anyone deaf and blind.

Chapter 2

WHY ME?

- Everyone who feels sick wants to know; at least 1.6 million U.S. polio survivors want to know; 500,000 want to turn the syndrome around as well as countless others with CFS
- Hypothesis: answers to chronic illness are illustrated in the pattern of life and medical histories of post polio survivors: in life styles and childhood illnesses.
- How the Type-A personality is an illness prone personality
- How the Sabin vaccines, DPT vaccine injuries, antibiotics, and meningitis may afford new clues to the problems
- Dr. Bruno's brain-leison discoveries: heat-cold regulator dysfunction, stress regulator dysfunction, weight regulator dysfunction, pain-control mechanism dysfunction, and sleep-wake regulator dysfunction. Unexamined assumption in research: did the damage preexist the PPS symptoms?
- How the maverick bad-tempered survivor works
- What the early polio-virus persistence hypothesis was and why there is something to it in many conditions
- What the Dr. Bodian findings in the forties were
- Dalakas's suspicious unidentified immune system activity surrounding damaged tissue
- My personal experience of taking the Salk vaccine after post polio syndrome was diagnosed
- Persistent virus infections have been proved in immune-weakened animals and children
- Hypothesis: weakened immune systems and poor nutrition cause polio and other chronic illnesses
- Only 1% of the U.S. population is susceptible to polio virus infection
- Why Magic Johnson will never get AIDS
- What the effects of vaccines are on increasing antibody production
- How weather and diet affect the syndrome
- How the syndrome of denial works when polio comes back to haunt you
- What the risks are of increasing activity to former levels when you feel good

Why me and 1.6 million Americans got polio in the first place is still on my mind and on the minds of at least another 500,000 post polio survivors who are now experiencing post polio syndrome: flu-like weakness,

5

chronic fatigue, pain, stiffness, increased instability and falling, excessive weight gain, accumulation of water in the tissues, depression, twitching muscles called fasciculations, difficulty in speaking, sleep disturbances, exercise intolerance, and inability to concentrate. Countless others have had similar symptoms diagnosed in England as Post Vaccination Syndrome; still others with the same symptoms are told they have Chronic Fatigue Syndrome; and still others are said to have Fibromyalgia. Whatever label you wish to place on it, everyone with chronic illness has one burning question. Why me? Why did it happen in the first place, and why is it still happening? Why is there so much illness in modern society? Why do we live longer but live weaker?

For polio survivors, it was bad enough once, and then it comes back. Many of the answers may lie hidden in the common ground that has already been illustrated in post polio survivors research, in CFS, and in others subject to serious illness. I suspect there is much more in common to be discovered by a comparative analysis of medical history and personality than would at first seem relevant. One area of common ground has been widely discussed in popular and medical literature about polio survivors. Most if not all the polio survivors were over-achieving, Type-A personalities before and after the acute phrase of the polio infection. I have an annoying suspicion that people subject to Post Polio Syndrome, Lupus, MS, Fibromyalgia, Alzheimer's, and other debilitating chronic illness are generally, if not universally, over-achievers. They are people who try harder than others to prove something because they might not have found easy social acceptance. The Type-A personality may be an illness-prone personality.

It would be equally valuable to discover if Type-A personalities are the ones still getting polio, not necessarily from environmental causes, but from the Sabin live-vaccine. Approximately twelve new cases of polio are reported each year in the United States. Most of these reported cases of acute polio infection come from the live strain of the virus in the Sabin vaccine. I suspect there are many more cases that go unreported simply because the people so infected believe that they have a bad case of the flu. Some epidemiologists have estimated that for every dose of live-vaccine administered that at least seven other people in the immediate family would contact polio from incidental contamination of fecal matter. My intent is not to call attention to the ethical issue of using the Sabin vaccine; the warning is posted on the brochures handed out for all to read who, of course, can read. Instead, my intent is to suggest a lifestyle, behavioral, possibly genetic predisposition to being susceptible to infection, with other childhood diseases that may play a part. Most people exposed to virus do not become sick. Long-lived people are not subject to common childhood illnesses. If the World Health Organization is right, what had been labeled polio infection was really spinal meningitis, caused not by the so-called polio virus, but by herpes virus. If this is true, there are not 12 people who could be studied but 12,012 people in 1992 alone. What do these people share in common? Are they Type-A personalities?

6

And what do the 250 deaths and the 7,200 adverse reactions to the DPT vaccinations in 1992 mean? As of November 16, 1992, *The Choice* (Fall 1992) reported that 3,000 claims have been filed against the U.S. government and the vaccine. Presumably most of us may be thankful that the 7,000 persons who usually died from contacting Whooping Cough as a natural infection was reduced to 7 in 1992. But as Dr. Joanne Hatem, medical director of the National Vaccine Information Center, said: "for an individual child, the risk is greater from the vaccine than from the disease." This is more than a little ominous. The DPT vaccine was introduced in the 1940s along with other vaccines against common illnesses. The dead Whooping Cough or Pertussis virus is believed to encourage antibody production. However, vaccines contain mercury compounds that, at the same time they preserve some things, act as neurotoxins for many individuals, 7,750 in 1992. Why are some people immediately harmed by the vaccines and not others? Are vaccinated people also people subject to chronic illness much later on?

Pertussis (Whooping Cough either through the disease itself or the vaccine), Candida, herpes zoster, the chicken pox and shingles viruses, may all play roles in chronic illness for reasons that will later become apparent.

To borrow an old description from an ancient medical journal: the people who got polio, and the people who are still getting polio and other serious illnesses, might just fall into the same category: Psychologically, they are hard workers, concentrators, stubborn, with a tendency never to give up. They work impatiently and impulsively until they are exhausted. They are easily affected emotionally with wide emotional swings in mood, easily angered and blow up in loud voices; then, the emotion is gone, and it is under control. They are good eaters. Physically, they experience accumulated fatigue due to never-ending drive; they are prone to overeating and other excesses with sweets and alcohol. They normally show swollen chests and stomachs. They experience headaches, poor digestion, dizziness, high fevers without apparent cause, chills, coughing, hemorrhoids, prostate problems, inflammation of the female reproductive organs, lower back pain, stiffness, flatulence, and inflammation.

Later, I want to explore where that came from, what theories of health it plays into and what some of the implications might be. Dr. Bruno discovered enough lesions in the hypothalamus of the brain in post polio tissue to believe that polio infection caused chronic illness: heat-cold regulator dysfunction, stress regulator dysfunction, fat metabolism dysfunction, susceptibility to addiction dysfunction, breathing and swallowing dysfunction, pain-control mechanism dysfunction, sleep-wake regulator dysfunction. All of this he assumed followed the polio infection, not preceded it. My point here is a suspicion: there may be a host of commonalities that polio survivors and others share that preexisted acute infections, so that not all of them may originate in a single virus or its sequelae, but in prior medical history, common childhood illnesses, common childhood vaccinations, the genetic makeup, behavioral habits, and general constitution of the groups who experience problems. Some of the damage noted in the muscles, brainstem, and spinal cords of post polio survivors may exist prior to the onslaught of acute polio infection, not after. Neurological damage is known to take place, for example, in some people who have been vaccinated. Excluded from biopsy studies of post polio spinal cords and other damaged tissue have been people who were known to have other conditions affecting their health, Alzheimer's disease, known exposure to toxins, Parkinson's disease, and other immune system and neuromuscular disorders. However, many undiagnosed neurological conditions might have been present in those who were autopsied. My father, for instance, went for years undiagnosed as having Alzheimer's. And even at the end of his life, he had been diagnosed as having many conditions that may have accounted for the debilitating neural, muscular, and mental problems he was afflicted with. Could it be that there are many factors that play a role in the disintegration and weakening of muscles and nerves and the regulation of hormonal factors that in turn affect neurotransmitters? I believe this to be the case. I also believe that a part of the problem in too much of the eighty pounds of research I've read on Post Polio Syndrome (PPS) problems has been to isolate: to find the single cause, to exclude other conditions, the very conditions that may have a bearing on the problem. Logically, isolating single causes is indefensible. It's known as an either-or fallacy or a false dilemma. Either overuse of surviving nerves caused it, or an unknown antigen or neurotoxin. Why not both and other factors in addition?

The collective makeup of PPS survivors may include a medical history profile all of us with chronic illness share in common, available in all of our medical charts, but not considered relevant to the syndromes and diseases we're presently diagnosed as having.

I'm convinced that the images that are burned into my memory from the polio ward suggest clues: A three year old, who was in the ward for a month, but who showed no visible signs of paralysis, used to stand up when he didn't care for something the nurse was doing to him, like administering those Sister Kinney, hot-steaming-wool hot packs, the smell of which still makes me gag and I suspect made the little tike more than gag. So when the hot packs arrived, he stood up and urinated all over the good nurse who was about to mummify him with scalding heat. That tike was the spitting image of Nash Jiminez, paralyzed in both legs, a 16-year-old, who taught me chess, algebra, and typing from a wheelchair. He was a Goliath physically and emotionally. He looked like an athlete sitting down and could have been mistaken for an Olympian hero at rest. He had the lung capacity of a long distance runner and the build of a wrestler. No one gave him any grief. When I made a stupid move in chess, Nash declared the beginning of World War III. Every polio patient in that ward was a potential cataclysm waiting its opportunity to happen. Their stress regulators had been transformed into life-and-death overreactions to small annoyances. When I

8

viewed Laura McCallum's, one of the founders of the Oregon Polio Survivors Association, account of her experience on video tape, I knew I was a member of a group who not only shared a set of symptoms but who also shared a great number of very strong personality characteristics, including a tendency to urinate on well-intentioned nurses bearing painful gifts and other people with medical authority whose gifts have included an innate talent that hides vast areas of unknowing. I met the same personality on Dr. Krakauer's video presentation of his interests in Eldepryl and his feeling that Parkinson's, Multiple Sclerosis, Alzheimer's, and other conditions may be closely related. It was the maverick in him and in her that I identified with, the one who would never quit, and who might seek for answers until exhausted.

As I waited for over a month to be diagnosed for Post Polio Syndrome, I read the book, *Research and Clinical Aspects of the Late Effects of Poliomyelitis, a collection of reports from the Second Symposium on the Late Effects of Poliomyelitis at Warm Springs,* California, 1986. I was struck by several things in reading that book as I waited, terrified that I might have the syndrome, and terrified that if I didn't I was probably dying on my feet. After all, cancer has been described by those who have experienced it as a flu from which you never recover. I thought I'd gotten the flu four months before, and I showed no signs of getting better. One of my friends thought I had AIDS. I had many of those symptoms too. One of my office mates suggested Multiple Sclerosis. Another, Alzheimer's, another hypochondria, another Chronic Fatigue Syndrome, another that I was just getting old. Well, strangely enough, I believed that they were all correct. Most of those illnesses shared much in common and felt like a flu that couldn't be shaken off.

The flu-like state I was in had lasted four months, and it was getting worse. Something had to be wrong.

One of the major theories explored in *Late Effects* was treatment based on Marinos C. Dalakas, M.D., Sever, Madden, and others, who had taken biopsies of spinal and muscle tissue only to find evidence that the exhaustive follow-up studies in the forties were apparently wrong. In 1945, Dr. Bodian had conducted intensive research and found no evidence that the polio virus continued as a persistent infection. It was gone from the system within three weeks after the initial acute infection. There were antibodies in the systems of post polio patients, but no living virus.

However, Dalakas in 1984, 1985, 1986, and 1988 found evidence of either new or persistent infectious or toxic activity. The old polio virus he theorized was reactivated, or some other toxin must be present to account for lymph activity surrounding nerve and muscle tissue. There was good evidence to suggest infection of some kind, but no evidence to suggest live polio virus, or some form of mutated polio virus. All of this was a surprise considering the exhaustive studies done in the 1940s where the presence of polio virus in people who had had polio years before had been given new

9

tests, and no polio virus was in evidence. Yet Dalakas found evidence of an unknown antigen. Viral, metallic toxin, or some other toxic agent, he theorized, had caused inflammation near nerve and muscle tissue in postmortem biopsies of tissue of PPS survivors who had died 5 to 40 years after the initial infection, an inflammation and immune mechanism activity that said SOMETHING toxic was causing it.

Clinical studies then cropped up, as reported in *Late Effects*, to administer Salk and/or Sabin vaccines to people experiencing symptoms. Of some surprise to me, was that the symptoms were reported to diminish if not disappear after the vaccine was taken. I had never taken the Salk vaccine. I got the initial acute polio infection in 1954, one year before Salk's vaccine was available, and no one had ever suggested taking the vaccine afterwards.

Of greater surprise to me was that when I was examined by an expert physiatrist, not psychiatrist, Physical Medicine M.D., and a person I highly respected and still do, this good physician simply said that all of the polio reactivation theory had been discounted. He no longer treated on that basis. Well, did that mean that the work of Dalakas and others was wrong? On no, no, not at all, there was very good evidence to suggest that what he found was in fact there. Well, did I get to have the Salk vaccine? He didn't use that as a part of his treatment. Well, would he give it to me anyway? The vaccine wasn't available in the hospital. Okay. Several sessions later, I was given further examination and electromyography study, all of which proved that I had evidence of new denervation, that nerves in previously unaffected parts of my body were now being affected. I was given very helpful advice in changing my lifestyle to conserve energy, to walk less, to change my classes so that the distance would be shorter, to get a handicap sticker, to sleep more, (a good trick in view of my insomnia), to do stretching exercises, all with the intent of reducing stress and energy expenditure based on the theory of OVERUSE, not on the theory of persistent infection or toxic activity of an unknown kind. Okay, I was logically suspicious that one treatment proving to be helpful was ignored. I was discouraged that no detoxification program was prescribed or even considered as an alternative.

The good physician invalidated a kind of treatment I both expected to receive and wanted to try. How could it hurt to get a booster of polio vaccine or a new series of shots? Just because it "wasn't currently accepted," translation—not the dominant or mainstream practice, it wouldn't be done. The authority structure and the emotional weight given to dominant attitudes seem to me both unrecognized by those within the group of authority and invisible except to those outside, namely me, and all other patients who run into the wall of authority, of frozen assumptions, and popular treatments. I don't mean to demean any person, and certainly not one who was both empathetic and sincere. But I do mean to highlight what others in research identify as "likemindedness." To suggest that there are other logical alternatives is to invite invalidation by the power structure of those presently in a majority position. All of this is both unconscious and nearly impossible to deal with since it's invisible to begin with. That's one of my motives in writing this book. I want to suggest alternatives to the mainstream, alternatives that work, if only for a limited period of time, even if the emotional electoral college didn't put them into office.

To learn from a Wall Street economist, "The majority is always wrong." If everyone believes the market is going up, it's sure to be headed in the opposite direction. Minority points of view can be right.

So I headed in an opposite direction, and with the support of a minority of one, me. I went right over to the Marion County Health department and started in on a new set of shots of the Salk polio vaccine. I asked the good doctor in charge if she would follow the protocol in the *Late Effects of Polio* book, gave her the book, since she hadn't, of course, even known much of anything about something called the post polio syndrome in the first place. She read the whole book. That was good. Two weeks later it was apparent to her that the protocol used by one clinic was not clear. It was also clear that most of the protocol involved the live Sabin vaccine, which also involved considerable risk in taking it. Later, I found out why. It immunizes most people; it actually causes serious paralytic polio, even death, in others.

As the brochure with the new live vaccines indicated, people in poor health should not even think about taking the shots. As Dalakas reported, animals with weakened immune systems not only get polio but evidence a history of continuing and persistent infection. And as Karen G. Holman, M.D., did not point out in "Post Polio Syndrome, the battle with the old foe resumes," human beings with weakened or compromised immune systems HAVE BEEN DEMONSTRATED TO SHOW SIGNS OF PERSISTENT INFECTION. Dr. Holman wrote, "persistent infection by the virus has been demonstrated in animals and has not been specifically excluded in humans." This disingenuous negative statement translates: persistent infection has been demonstrated in humans with compromised immune systems. In fact, in Johnson, RT, Lazzarini RA, and Waksman, BH: Mechanisms of virus persistence, *Ann Neurol* 1981; 9:590-596, Davis, LF, Bodian, D, Price DL, et al: Chronic progressive poliomyelitis secondary to vaccination of an immunodeficient child, *N Engl J Med* 1977; 297:241-248, and Miller, JR: Prolonged intracerebral infection with poliovirus in asymptomatic mice, *Ann Neurol* 1981; 9:590-596, all demonstrate persistent infection when weakened immune systems pre-exist the polio infection.

Mice with weakened immune systems were demonstrated to show persistent infection that didn't go away; a child with a weakened immune system never got rid of the infection. Could it be that what set us all up to get polio in the first place was (1) some form of weakened immune system (2) poor health including poor nutrition? I ask this because only 1%, that's one percent, of all people exposed to the virus actually come down with

11

infection. That's a very small group out of a very large population. And is the same set of causes continuing to weaken those of us with chronic illness?

I can't help but think of Magic Johnson, the world-famous basket ball player. He tested HIV positive. He has the virus in his system that is alleged to cause AIDS, autoimmune deficiency, yet he has not developed any of the signs of AIDS. Others who have been exposed to the HIV virus, who have been otherwise in good health, don't develop AIDS. Are those people who come down with full-blown AIDS members of a very small group who share similar lifestyles and dietary histories with post polio survivors? Similar medical histories as others who come down with Parkinson's and Lupus?

In some doctors logically rushing through this issue, I believe the dominant majority position INVALIDATED THE DEMONSTRATION THAT ONE, ONE GROUP DID SHOW PERSISTENT INFECTION. That group, may just compose a part of the 20% of the post polio survivors, those subject to Chronic Fatigue Syndrome, and many other chronic illnesses where slow infections are implicated. Why should one treatment serve for all? The ounce of prevention that MIGHT produce a pound of improvement for even one person WOULD be worth it for that one person I assure you, if you were that one person. Did I want the live Sabin vaccine that was even recognized as dangerous for otherwise healthy young adults? In no way did I want to take that on. I may have been one of those with a compromised or weakened immune system. Did I still want the booster shots of the dead virus that promised to boost my antibody count? Did I want to stupidly ignore further potential neurological damage from the neurotoxins in the vaccine? Considering that life was not worth living, yes, I did, and I got them for five bucks a shot.

Did I experience any effects from the shots that I was subjectively aware of? Good question. There were changes, but I also followed the advice of the Physical Medicine Unit of the hospital I went to. The first change I noticed was that I slept better. And I slept better with copious night sweating. I'd wake up at first absolutely drenched with sweat. But the rest I could get from sleep gradually lengthened. Did I improve because of the vaccine, the rest, the conservation of energy, my changing my lifestyle to something less active, or did the fact that I could sleep turn things around for a few months? Do vaccine antibodies not only afford protection against the disease they're supposed to, but also give protection against viral cousins? The obvious answer is: all of the above, or part of the above. Taking vaccines is believed to encourage antibody production generally. Of course, there is a risk from the mercury preservative used in vaccines. And mercury is a neurotoxin. But at the time, I wanted to take the risk. I couldn't sit around and do nothing.

My dominant complaint at the time of a PPS diagnosis was lack of energy and strength. Chronic pains, contrary to other reports, were not problematic to me. I had the pains, but they were not the important issue. The important thing to me was that I had no energy whatsoever to do things. I wanted to do things, pain or no pain.

In the course of six months, I gradually improved with the weather. The worst of the symptoms had come on in the fall, got worse in the winter, and improved with rising temperatures in the spring. They continued to improve throughout the warm summer and an unusually warm and sunny fall in Oregon into the next year. Then, as the temperatures declined so did my energy and strength. By winter, I was a basket case. I knew things were coming back, but I practiced vigorous denial. This was not happening to me. I refused to accept the fact that things were getting worse until they were so bad I had to try something new. Did they get worse because, as I felt better, I gradually increased my activity levels to my normal manic assault on the impossible? Was the weather more responsible than anything else for problems and alleviation of problems? Are there whole population studies that exist for cold and warm regions of a country that include chronic illness? If there were, the *Weekly Mobidity and Mortality Report* had not found them. The International Polio Network had published a world directory of support groups though: 26 groups in Canada compared with one in Israel did suggest cold regions had greater problems. It would be fascinating to discover that illness hates warmth and sunshine.

Had I tried anything new during the months I experienced improvements? All of the above may afford clues.

I'm convinced that weather is a factor.

Increasing activity to overwork because you feel better is a factor. I was always a work horse and couldn't relax when I was relaxing. I could only relax when I was under fire. That old strategy was no longer working, but I persisted in following it.

I had also tried alternative treatments during the course of my improvements, and I continued them until I felt better. I put my finger in the hole that developed in the dike for that day; when the water stopped leaking, I pulled my finger out. I had stopped doing some of the things that had been helping and wouldn't try them again until I felt like dropping dead. I cultivated a stoic response to pain; it was part of the old-world cultural baggage I carried so deeply inside that even I didn't know it was there. Even I didn't know it was there. Polio had made me super conscious of my body, and a part of that inwardness was directed at keeping me in touch with both the condition of my physical body and the currents in my mind. When my left leg was paralyzed, walking became a conscious act. I believed that nearly everything else in me had become conscious too. Nearly everything.

People with illness do become so hyperconscious that those who live around them accuse them of hypochondria, unfairly, of course.

Chapter 3

ONE ALTERNATIVE: CHIROPRACTIC, OSTEOPATHY, NATUROPATHY

- Holistic theory: skeletal, blood, nervous system, and lifestyle are treated together
- Holistic assumption: the body knows how to heal itself; disease is a symptom of toxins and imbalances the body created by lifestyle and unmanaged stresses
- Lifestyle, attitudes, and stress disease are a part of holistic operating assumptions
- What stress seeking and stress intolerance is like in chronic illness
- What the AMA says about conserving energy
- How attitudes about physical health are treated differently by chiropractic
- How I experienced slow improvements with chiropractic and massage
- How to improve your diet
- Why chiropractic, massage, acupuncture, and orthodox medicine should be integrated
- Salix alba and chinchona officinalis: herbal muscle-relaxant alternatives to pain-killing drugs
- Quinine pro and con
- Conflicting health professional attitudes: use it and lose it; use it or lose it; common sense and compromises
- Either-or life fallacies
- Susceptibility to addiction in PPS: cautions for drug dependencies with damaged nerves
- My early and later experiences of herbal KM: potassium and energy
- How Type-A's get right back into overwork patterns and get into trouble
- How to learn to slow down even if it kills an old self image
- What supplements and food can do for you
- What role potassium plays in chronic illness from dry skin to fatigued muscles
- Suspicion: sleepwalkers and restless sleep and acetylcholine
- The Candida hypothesis: silent infections precede chronic illness
- How to feed your overworked nerves
- Why you should take calcium for muscle cramps and twitches

15

- How talking nutrition might not get you anywhere with doctors not required to take courses in clinical nutrition
- How soft drinks and coffee affect magnesium, phosphorus, manganese
- Magnesium deficiencies: low blood sugar, poor energy, bad temper, nervousness, tremors; depression, prostate problems, tooth decay, overweight
- Why you should have a mineral analysis
- Caution: pain killers lower body temperature
- Some common sense strategies to cope with cold weather
- Why Vitamin D can be taken for depression and Growth Hormone production
- How sunshine relieves pain: chemical sunshine, the pineal and pituitary
- What emotional hibernation and bears have in common
- The herbalist view of what causes polio, nerve disease, and most major illnesses
- Stresses and habits that malnourish: the Type-A pattern

When I complained to a friend of Post Polio Syndrome symptoms, I was advised to try a chiropractic physician in Salem, Oregon, simply because she was reported to "work wonders" with chronic conditions and to be able to figure out "anything." With a recommendation like that, I couldn't resist.

Before I was treated, I was asked to fill out an exhaustive medical history and a full set of my current symptoms. I was immediately impressed with the questionnaire, since my symptoms and the symptoms of chronic illness in general were all listed on the form. How could a method of medicine know in advance all those things that were new information to other members of the medical profession? Maybe I was convinced before I started that I may have happened into the right hands. After all, if the form has your name written all over it, maybe you were in the right place.

During my first treatment, I was told that when my symptoms were added up that the intensity of my unhealthy state was off the scale in all areas: physical skeletal system, blood system, and nervous system. I was very stiff and unaware of it. I had pains everywhere I was touched, and I had been unaware of that. I had blocked them out. I was advised to get a whole body massage from a licensed masseuse just to loosen me up enough to work on. I felt like my back was made of steel. Then, I was treated twice a week for a month or so. Then, I was treated once a week. Then, once a month, and I stopped treatments after I felt good.

One of the first things I learned was that the brand of chiropractic I was given was holistic. Many of its methods dated back to Hippocrates in 400

B.C. and was founded on a number of very old assumptions, used for thousands of years.

Assumption number one: the body has an inborn intelligence and knows how to heal itself.

Assumption two: Symptoms of diseased states are manifestations of the body's vital force trying to right itself by the removal of toxins, stresses and imbalances in the physical body.

This assumption in itself was reassuring; Dalakas and others had already found that an unknown toxin was inflaming the nervous system and muscles, that postural deformities placed undue stress on nerves, joints and muscles, and all of it was presumably started by an acute polio infection that, when one limb was paralyzed, had destroyed 20% of the then existing neurons. The surviving neurons were then, you might say, subject not only to an imbalance, but a necessary overload to carry on nearly normal everyday functions.

Assumption three: The causes and effects of diseased states are not simply confined to a single location like the spine, or the brain, but arise out of a whole lifestyle, a whole constellation of causes, previous medical history, reactions to stress, general bodily health, all of which interact.

Reaction to stress was very provocative to me. Most of my adult life was characterized by a high toleration to stress. I sought it out, I created it for myself, and I thrived on it. Suddenly, I found that changing. I could no longer tolerate it, I didn't seek to set up situations that provoked it, and I avoided it whenever possible. I was quiet when I normally would have spoken up, all to avoid trouble. I had been told by the physiatrist to cut down on stress by cutting down on the physical stress I was placing on my body by walking less, resting more, working less, and making my seated posture and walking posture as upright as possible. In my emotional life, that was exactly what my feelings were telling me. Cut down on the emotional stresses as well.

I would never have made this kind of connection of my mental life with physical problems had it not been for a chiropractic physician who encouraged me to talk about my feelings and to look at how I was handling everyday situations. As my attitudes improved, so did my "feelings" of physical health. And the other way around, my physical health improved my attitudes.

Over a month's period of time, I was seen two times a week, massaged to loosen tight areas, given material to read about health and nutrition, encouraged to seek out answers, had my neck and spine adjusted, and given herbal treatments. Maybe more than anything else, I valued the talk about what stresses were taking place in my life and how I handled them. Body and mind were part of the treatment.

A month into the treatments, I might have felt a fraction of a hair better. I heard people in the chiropractor's office absolutely bubbling with responses to the same herbal preparations I was taking, and I was envious that I didn't feel as vital and alive as they did. I had to count my improvements in crumbs. But as the winter wore on, my posture was improving with stretching and adjustment, massage, and herbal assistance that, in two more months' time, began to feel miraculous. I had been told that natural herbal medications acted very differently from drugs. They worked slowly; they built up in one's system over a long period of time; they remained in the system for a lengthy period of time; and slowly but surely they would work. They were also non-toxic. There were no side effects; healthy tissue would not be damaged, and weak tissue would be strengthened.

At least two approaches to therapy coincided: The physical medicine approach emphasized ameliorating postural stress by stretching to make my legs nearly vertical again, paying attention to my posture in sitting, and the chiropractic approach which helped set my posture more upright by relieving the stress on my vertebrae. Both suggested taking care with sitting positions, adjusting the level of the work space (the desk in my case), using a small back cushion, all with the intent of relieving stress on muscles and joints. As the tensions were relieved, my energy began to return; my pain levels decreased; and my sleeping was less disturbed.

I was also encouraged to improve my nutrition with whole grains, twelve whole-grain breads and whole-grain cereals, more fruit and vegetables in my diet. I was introduced to high-energy snacks for the first time in my life, nuts, dried fruit, vegetables, an orange in between meals, all with noticeably positive effects on my energy.

It was pointed out by physical medicine oriented studies in the *Journal of the American Medical Association* that postural deformities such as scoliosis, an S-curvature of the spine, may entrap nerves, injure nerves, and encourage fatigue for post polio people. My wife had such an S-curve in her spine, and she like others of our friends experienced chronic problems. Chiropractic seems like it should be an obvious member of a team approach to manage PPS and chronic illness. Could apparently competing medical approaches be integrated because of their obvious complementary nature? As Allen Taylor pointed out to me, that integration has already taken place in sports medicine. Why? The players ask for it. I am asking for such an integration.

With or without such an integration from a professional point of view, it seems to me that it is an approach well worth trying from the patient's initiative and choice.

Two herbal preparations are worthy of note as a part of the approach I was introduced to. My chiropractor was versed in naturopathic and homeopathic information. One is by brand name known as 7-R, an herbal combination of Salix alba and Cinchona officinalis, or more commonly known as willow bark (the herbal origin of aspirin) and the herbal origin of the extract, quinine. It may have taken two bottles' worth before I experi-

18

enced any effects, but the effects were close to the miracles that weren't supposed to exist in this life.

Margaret Krieg's *Green Medicine* helped explain to me why the herbal parent of quinine was working. Quinine alkaloids have a long history of medical uses in treating rapid heart rates, relieving muscle cramps, fever and respiratory infections, and have a muscle relaxant curare-like effect in relieving headaches, joint and muscle disorders. But in its extract form, it has been known too for hundreds of years to have unfortunate side effects when taken in large quantities, even causing deafness and death. But in its herbal form as a bark of the Chinchona tree known as Peruvian Bark for the country of its origin, it is non-toxic with no side effects. Combined with willow bark, it seems like a perfect alternative to more powerful and more fast-acting painkillers and anti-inflammatory drugs. It's not fast, but it doesn't injure stomach linings or kidneys either.

Over a period of two months, I began to feel relaxed everywhere, experienced less pain and stiffness, and could tolerate much more emotional stress. I felt better all over, and I began to seek out stressful activities again, challenging my peers, my students, and myself. All of this was made possible by an alternative approach added to the medical profession's suggestions about reducing activity and conserving energy.

It seems unfortunate that antagonisms exist between alternative health care approaches and American Medical Association approaches. Some considerable new stress was experienced when I took advantage of both. For one thing, I heard the attitude that "you will gradually get worse," "sickness is normal," and "we can make the benign progression of worsening symptoms" a little easier on you from the AMA attitudes. I heard something equally anxiety-producing from the chiropractic side of things: health is a natural state. If you're not healthy, you're not right. If you save yourself for another day, that day may never come. I was not encouraged to conserve energy from the chiropractic point of view. I was encouraged to get back with it.

On the one hand, I was told to get in a wheelchair by my M.D. if I wanted to slow the progression of the disease; and on the other, I was told that if I got in a wheelchair, I'd never get out.

I found both extremes distressing. I was caught in another either-or life fallacy. Either you should be totally healthy, or resign yourself to total sickness. I was somewhere in between. So I pursued the middle course, my course, with a slight imbalance towards overdoing things. I rested more; I did more. I used the wheelchair, and I walked. I tried to find a balance appropriate for me. But one thing is certain to my mind: herbal treatments can be helpful to bettering the syndrome no matter what you do or what balance you try to achieve.

Willow bark is the original herbal source of aspirin; Cinchona officinalis is the herbal origin of quinine. In combination, and over a period of time, I felt better and better physically and emotionally. As my body felt better, my depression went away. Towards the end of the second bottle, I'd say that I felt damned ecstatic. Ecstatic, Dr. Guruka Khalsa said. It's a normal state; you can feel that way without the herbs. It's known as health.

Oh? Maybe during warm weather and sunshine.

I was pain free for a change though and it was winter, and I was on top of the heap with a little help from herbs, massage, and freeing up some entrapped nerves.

Soma and other drug therapies have been mentioned in American Medical Association literature and in PPS newsletters. Soma has been prescribed as a muscle relaxant with some hesitancy and some fear of dependency for reasons that haven't been all that clearly stated in most places. PPS survivors are VERY susceptible to addiction because the part of the hypothalamus that regulates natural pain killer production of endorphins and enkephalins has been damaged by the polio virus or something else. Aspirin and other anti-inflammatory drugs have also been prescribed for obvious reasons. I've tried them all.

7-R as a natural alternative has none of the hazards to either stomach or kidneys or central nervous system that aspirin, Tylenol 3, (a narcotic pain killer), Darvon, Darvocette, Advil, all of which I've tried, and all of which work to block pain and reduce inflammation. 7-R is not only non-addictive (I stopped using it for months during warm weather and forgot about it for instance), it doesn't irritate any healthy tissue.

KM: KM is also an herbal preparation with two dozen herbal tinctures, not extracts, the dominant one of which gives it its name, the chemical symbol for potassium. Its formula was developed to help restore energy and general vitality. And it too was slow on having any noticeable effect on me. However, four months after beginning to take KM, I was bursting with energy, so much so that my boss started me in on what must have precipitated my next regression into Nowheresville debilitating pain, fatigue, and nothingness. Anyway, KM worked successfully to restore me to previous levels of energy, strength, and yes, vitality. I began once again feeling good, I spoke up as I usually did, and I got into tons of extra work because of it, extra projects, extra committee work, extra consulting for my employer.

The Boss: It's impossible to fix.

PPS Me: Well, maybe this will work to fix it.

The Boss: You brought it up; you do it.

PPS survivors and others prone to overwork should learn to shut up, and more importantly to say no. The word, no, was not a part of my vocabulary. There is a great danger once you have a good day, or week, or month, to return to abnormal levels of energy expenditure that will land you right back in trouble. Type-A's willingness to try the impossible is part of the disease, not the cure. That high level of energy lasted precisely six months. I went right back to bad habits of overwork, walking too much, too far, sitting too long, and not getting enough rest and sleep. I stopped pacing myself.

All the warnings are in the advice of AMA physicians, literature, and newsletters. I think it's a warning well worth paying attention to for many people with overwork stresses in their lives. Chronic-illness syndromes may be precipitated by the very personality makeup, the overdoing-it lifestyle of Type-A personalities. Learn to slow down and smell the roses even if it kills you. It won't. It will kill an old self image, and you will have to mourn its passing for awhile. Mourn it infrequently: it's too painful to remember, and it is an illusion that you are honoring. But you will discover something much better. Less really is more: pacing, lesser activity, two hours of rest during the day, and nine to ten hours of sleep or rest at night are essential, you might even say civilized.

As I look back on it now, and I know a little bit about potassium, I think I know why KM or a potassium supplement can be helpful. For one thing, it's an essential mineral nutrient found in food sources in fruit, in legumes, in red cabbage, dates, figs, dried apricots, baked potatoes, and tomatoes in significant concentrations. My diet had rarely included any of those foods except for an occasional baked potato, and seasonally, tomatoes in the summer when they look and taste like tomatoes. There was far too much meat and fat in my diet, and way too little of fruit and vegetables of any kind. Fruits and vegetables are the main sources of potassium, anti-cancer diets, anti-heart disease diets, and good health. Where we used to eat bushels of apples in the 19th century, it is rare to eat a dozen a year now.

What does potassium do?

Nearly everyone knows it's important for strengthening the heart muscle. But I didn't know it was important for maintaining all muscles and nerve health. Typical deficiency symptoms are: dry skin (mentioned in the *Handbook on the Late Effects of Poliomyelitis for Physicians and Survivors* as a common condition of a PPS person's skin), high blood pressure (which I had, 150 over 100), general weakness (which all PPS people share with many others), muscle damage (which 20 to 80% of post polio people may eventually be bothered with), nervousness (mine was world class), and insomnia (mine was right up there with the all-time greats).

I do know that potassium is an electrolyte, as is common old everyday table salt, and is essential for nerve impulse transmission, and in one study not only facilitates proper muscle contraction, but also promotes a healthy relaxed muscle. Somehow, potassium both makes the muscle work, and it helps it rest. Are low-sodium diets helping to precipitate poor muscular health in people? Have we removed the salt from the table and not included vegetables on the plate?

The muscle twitching or tics that I've had for as long as I remember in my good right leg, called fasciculations technically, a flickering of random

21

muscular contractions that is totally involuntary, I know is a symptom of nerve disease or nerve and muscular damage. At no time did those twitchings ever diminish with or without potassium. It was explained to me by Dr. David R. Cooper that hypertrophied axons, the super size of the surviving nerves in the spinal cord which took over to compensate for nerves destroyed by polio, those superman and superwoman sized axons begin to become over-efficient and send out more signals than necessary. In fact, they may be continuously firing. They are never shut off in my experience of waking or insomnia. They always make my muscles twitch day and night, contributing to overworked nerves, overworked muscles, and fatigue.

Part of this pattern of overwork is caused by a faulty sleep-wake mechanism which does not turn off impulses to the muscles, not in the spinal cord, but in the brain itself.

Dr. Richard Bruno found that the brain's sleep-wake mechanism is damaged in PPS survivors, and I wouldn't be surprised if similar areas of injury would be found to exist in others with chronic illness. He found lesions in many areas of the brain, a pinholed, or "Swiss-cheesed" effect, in the hypothalamus and the brain stem. The sleep-wake mechanism has holes in it. Other symptoms of a faulty sleep-wake mechanism involve sleepwalking or restless sleep. In a properly functioning sleep-wake mechanism, impulses are shut off to the muscles during sleep. Sleepwalking is an extreme form of impulses not being shut off. I was one of the sleepwalkers before I got polio, and I wonder how many others predisposed to chronic illness have the same history. The damage Dr. Bruno found may exist prior to the acute polio infection and be worsened by the polio virus itself. And I now believe, as will be discussed later, it is worsened further by pseudoinfection and an innocent seeming omnipresent yeast infection. Years worth of cellular and microbe waste may be the triggering mechanism for our autoimmune systems attacking our tissues, our brains, our spinal cords, our muscles, our organs. And if Dr. Richard Murray is correct, unfriendly bugs too are attracted to sites of injury, causing worse injury after the fact. Sites of injury may be chemically marked with aldehydes, accumulations of our own body's wastes.

In part, the fasciculations blamed on hypertrophied spinal nerves in PPS may be a sign of the nerve impulses not shutting off from the brain's faulty regulator, both before and after polio, worsening further as people age.

It makes some sense to me that if nerves won't rest, they'd better be given a little more nutrition to live on, to nourish and sustain the system. The twitches may never go away, but at least they will have enough electrolytic nutrition to keep them going on a mineral level.

As potassium plays a role in this nerve nutrition, the same may be said for calcium and magnesium. **Calcium** has been sometimes mentioned as an aid in reducing muscular cramping that limbs experience when they are subject to PPS even though it may be a surprise to many experts on PPS:

the experts who hand out the articles on such things might not have mentally registered the information. I received such a handout, but it was an invisible kind of footnote in the PPS literature. Perhaps, my old college friend, Bill Steines, now an M.D. and radiologist, was right. He said he'd been given one hour of nutritional instruction at USC as a student. It was never considered important enough to emphasize. Maybe the attitude was learned much more than the scanty information for the 5% of the MDs who chose to take one elective course in diet and nutrition. The four food groups were plenty to give lip service to in passing. It's an old and persistent attitude. At the turn of the 20th century and earlier, emphasis on nutrition was removed from the medical curriculum and relegated to the homeopaths and naturopaths. An emphasis on drug therapy replaced it for the American Medical Association. Medicine became drug therapy. So I'd say M.D.s are not to be blamed for not thinking it important. It was never made important in their schooling. Trying to discuss nutrition or vitamins with an M.D. is to run into an affective barrier, a wall of negative attitudes, and a canyon of yawning.

Each time I'd find a mineral or vitamin or amino acid that helped me regain a fraction of good health, I'd make the mistake of discussing it with an M.D. Little did I know at the time that the M.D.s knew less than I did.

Magnesium, well, you get enough in your diet.

Magnesium makes calcium more easily assimilated by the body and is another essential mineral nutrient for nerves. So are **phosphorus** and **manganese**. In fact, magnesium may be the control center for mineral metabolism. In many people like me, it was not an important ingredient in my diet. Also in too many people like me, coffee and soft drinks aggravate the deficiency. You may not hear that from your family physician. But William Crook, M.D., quotes experts in the field as saying that caffeinated beverages and phosphate containing soft drinks are mineral wasters. As a kid prior to getting polio, I was a soft drink addict. As an adult, coffee has been my favorite beverage. It was my father's favorite from early morning to late evening, and he ended his life unable to walk, speak, or feed himself.

The case for magnesium: normal blood sugar levels are facilitated by adequate magnesium levels, energy metabolism, calcium and vitamin C metabolism. Magnesium deficiencies show up behaviorally in easily aroused anger (I have the shortest fuse on record), nervousness and tremors. These were also my father's problems although they were blamed on Alzheimer's and sometimes on personality. The internist I first visited pointed out the tremors; he neglected to point out how it might be remedied by diet. Bad temper was not on his list of symptoms.

Of course, medical histories of post polio survivors with the syndrome usually mention bad temper or poor stress regulation. The shortest fuses on record may be directly tied to magnesium deficiencies.

Other magnesium deficiency symptoms are revealing: depression (oh?), nervousness, prostate troubles (I've had them), tooth decay (I've been single handedly responsible for putting three of my dentist's children through college), and overweight (I thought it was the shrinking effect of hot water on my clothes). With the exception of prostate and tooth problems, the rest are well-known PPS symptoms. If a full, collective medical history were compiled, I'd put money on the other two problems showing up in PPS survivors and others with chronic illness.

No blood or hair analysis was ever performed to check me for mineral or vitamin deficiencies by any doctor. Were it possible to do all over again, I would insist on such tests from the beginning. If this report lands on friendly survivors' ears and professional medical ears, I hope such tests will be performed on chronic-illness people before their symptoms improve to see if that really is a factor that can be established once and for all. In *The Betrayal of Health,* by Dr. Joseph Beasley, mineral deficiencies began showing up in the first national surveys of the seventies. *The Well Mind Association* newsletters from 1987 on have reported studies of criminals, Alzheimer's, Parkinson's, and children with learning disabilities that show mineral deficiencies and unusual excesses of copper, lead, cadmium, mercury, aluminum. I started taking supplements months before I had a hair analysis, and I still came up short in magnesium, calcium, potassium, and all trace minerals.

Dr. Bruno found that the cold-heat regulation section of the hypothalamus was also injured in PPS survivors. Cold feet, cold limbs, reduce circulation and nerve efficiency. While painkillers like aspirin reduce pain, they also reduce body temperature. You can be cold in a warm room. Bruno has pointed out that cold weather reduces PPS manual dexterity. And it only takes a drop in temperature to 68 degrees Fahrenheit to experience the problem. I think cold also plays an important role in increased falling, stumbling, and general clumsiness. Winter has always been the absolute worst for all PPS symptoms rising. In Oregon where I live, it's cold, damp, and frequently without sunshine. Sunshine is the only sure precursor for adequate **vitamin D**, and calcium can't be utilized in the body without it. Coldness, dampness, and darkness play an important role in aggravating PPS problems; they also play a role in encouraging fungal infections. Some common sense strategies are: raising the temperature in the house or workplace, wearing thermal underwear, using heating blankets, turning on more lights, and generally wearing warmer clothing.

A long winter vacation in the sunshine or permanent relocation are things worth thinking about. My acupuncturist was the first to point that out to me. And I believe she was more right on that issue than she will ever know. Her observations were based on the ancient world view that divides the universe into four basic elements: fire, air, earth and water. When they are balanced inside and out, you are healthy. When they are not, you are not. She said innocently one day, "Do you live in a dark and damp house?"

Yep, I live in Oregon. And I've seen countless Canadians at seminars who have only experienced two hours of faint sunshine in six months. They don't look good and they don't feel well.

I think supplemental **vitamin D** may play an important role in making winter take less of a toll. Cold weather may reduce PPS manual dexterity and gross muscular strength, but cold weather also accompanies lack of sunshine. When there is light under an Oregon monsoon, there is less of it because of the season. Dr. Bruno has pointed out that a non-Arctic 68 degrees Fahrenheit is all it takes to begin to lose strength and dexterity if you're subject to PPS. The cause may be located in lesions he believes were caused by the polio's insidious work on the hypothalamus. The cold and heat regulator is knocked out; and the pituitary may be impaired. Vitamin D may help restore some of the pituitary's normal functioning.

The pituitary? The size of a pea, it's your seasonal adjustment center and, together with its companion pea-sized pineal gland, it is light sensitive. It secretes a number of hormones important in tissue maintenance and repair (GH), stress regulation, fat metabolism, and stores other hormones produced by the hypothalamus.

One of my long term suspicions since leaving California has been and continues to be that lack of sunshine also influences pain levels, general feelings of well being, energy and everything else. The lack of sunshine as every Oregonian who does not thrive on the underside of a rock knows is that when the cloud comes over and the monsoons begin, so does depression. SAD or Seasonal Affective Disorder is well known in Oregon and follows less exposure to sunlight. What may not be well known is that vitamin D is not only produced by the effect of sunshine on the skin, but it is important to maintain the nervous system. The maintenance of the nervous system and depression are linked to the sun. This may account for the incidence of schizophrenia, alcoholism, and other chronic illness in Native Americans from the Northwest and Scandinavians who deviate from their traditional diets of salmon. Salmon is full of vitamin D and may have compensated for lack of sunshine in northern climates.

To my way of thinking, vitamin D is chemical sunshine. Insomnia, nervousness, and poor metabolism can be the result of vitamin D deficiency. All of these states are regulated by the pituitary and the pineal. So I say for those like me who don't have the money to move into the sunshine, I say bring on the cod liver oil, the salmon, and the liver. I'll take the supplements for vitamin D and gorge on salmon.

There are studies that link depression to a faulty sleep-wake clock mechanism. I haven't found any studies that link vitamin D to this mechanism or to seasonal depression in humans, but I did find a fascinating study on bears who hibernate that suggests a link. If vitamin D is injected into a hibernating bear, the bear does not hibernate. As far as I'm concerned, one of my basic impressions of depression is that I've felt asleep when I should have been awake. I was emotionally hibernating. The sleep-wake regulator was known to be out of kilter by Dr. Bruno; I propose that chemical sunshine may play an important role in righting it. I take cod liver oil now and rarely have insomnia. I'm annoyingly cheerful.

And I think I know why birds don't migrate when their pineal glands are surgically removed. The pineal is light sensitive; it orients birds to the sun and stars, south in winter, north in spring, as demonstrated in studies given in *The Parable of the Beast*, by John Bleibtreu. People with chronic illness may not have their pineals or pituitaries removed, but they may not be working right either. It might be of some interest to look at what was believed to result from mineral deficiencies alone from the standard reference book to herbal medicine since 1939, by Jethro Kloss, *Back to Eden:*

"Deficiency Diseases

"You cannot get mineral supply for your body from pills or bottles but out of natural foods the way nature prepares them.

"God in his infinite wisdom neglected nothing, and if we would eat our food without trying to improve, change, and refine it, thereby destroying its life-giving elements, it would meet all the requirements of the body.

"Diseases Caused by a Deficiency of Minerals (I won't list them all)

Anemia	Heart Disease
Cancer	Rickets
Diabetes	Scurvy
Eczema	Tuberculosis
Malnutrition	'Nerves'
Neuralgia	Neuritis
Paralysis	Infantile paralysis
Sciatica	Skin eruptions"

I took particular note of infantile paralysis and other diseases of the nervous system. Most other serious illnesses are listed as well. Could a predisposition to polio and other serious illnesses be caused by, can we say, the lifestyle of Type-A personalities who don't pay attention to their diet? Have we eaten too much industrialized food where transportation, storage, cooking, and freezing have removed what nature put in there in the first place?

We don't eat right for many reasons. We drink too many beverages with caffeine. We consume too many soft drinks. We unknowingly give refuge to a colony of yeast because of our diet.

Stress depletes some of the nutrients. Other stresses are caused by lack of nutrients. By nutritional deprivation, we may have slowly injured our tissues, triggering our own immune systems to digest what they considered damaged tissue. Foreign microbes may have been attracted by the same smells of damage. Since we live in the fast lane, we eat too many fast overly processed foods to rush back to overwork to rush through dinner to rush to oblivion. Lifestyle and personality may set us up for illness in the first place; and as we age, lifestyle and personality may not allow us to slow down long enough to figure out what's going wrong and how we could make it right.

Chapter 4

THE UNKNOWN BUG AND L-LYSINE

- Do we have flu or flu-like weakness?
- What autopsy reports revealed about lack of nerve nutrients and signs of infection
- Why chickenpox, polio, and other motor neuron disease may be related: scarring on the skin and brain
- Why chickenpox is a candidate for polio's, meningitis's, and chronic illness's viral parent
- What Ebola Reston, Zaire, Marburg and their evolution from friendly to fatal; fatal to friendly suggests about chronic slow infections in polio, Chronic Fatigue Syndrome, AIDS
- How pleomorphism can explain the slow infection theory and why a virus has not been detected
- How evolution of virus from fatal to annoying may create a debilitating persistence of chronic illness
- How early research analogies suggest a literal truth about chickenpox and herpes as polio's, shingles', and meningitis's parent
- How treating shingles with L-lysine relieved pain and improved concentration
- Foods and virus encouragement; foods and virus inhibition
- Lysine, carnitine, energy, concentration, weight loss and Alzheimer's
- Treating your weight control center with lysine
- How known lysine deficiencies of fatigue, nausea, dizziness, anemia suggest a dietary player in chronic illness
- What dosages of lysine have been used in clinical studies
- How you can inhibit an unknown slow-virus infection no matter what it is
- How a doctor's diagnosis and initial treatment of pertussis and candida infection began to clear up problems in concentration and chronic coughing
- How pertussis takes up residence in the mucous membranes but not the blood
- How pertussis could be hiding in the spine and brain
- How pertussis and swallowing and breathing difficulties in PPS may be related
- Where Candida is found: kinds of infection (mouth, skin, vaginal, intestinal, nails, systemic)
- How antibiotics, birth control pills, steroids, chemotherapy act as triggering mechanisms for immune disorders and Candida albicans infection

- My experience with caprylic acid for Candida and partial remission of symptoms
- How neurotransmitter disruption and Candida are related
- My early Candida hypothesis for PPS and other chronic illness
- How treatments for Candida have caused remission of Multiple Sclerosis, Lupus, and other autoimmune diseases
- What the symptoms of Candida infection are: THEY ARE NOT COMMONLY KNOWN BY DOCTORS OR ANYONE ELSE
- How Candida depresses the immune system
- What illnesses Candida is known to mimic: MS, hemolytic anemia, Crohn's disease, and Lupus remissions when Candida has been treated
- How Candida's acetaldehydes pickle tissue, muscles, Central Nervous System, and brain
- How Candida may be responsible for pseudoinfection or slow infection
- What Candida's likely effects on the brain and spinal cords of PPS survivors, MS, Parkinson's, and Alzheimer's are and what they have been confused with
- How the triggering mechanism of Candida's by-products work
- How allergy attacks and Candida are related
- How drunken white blood cells may start autoimmune attacks on our brains, CNS, and muscles
- How Candida's episodic nature and chronic illness's episodic pattern are related
- How chronic illness was placed in early remission with Candida treatment in the author
- Why you should give Candida competition with L. acidophilus
- How Candida and cold, damp weather are linked
- What in your diet encourages Candida growth
- How Candida can be connected with strange tastes in your mouth
- What Candida explains about why you don't like perfume or cologne
- Why many unanswered questions need further study
- Why people with chronic illness stopped complaining to their doctors and other habits of denial
- How Candida runs in the family

If it feels like the flu and acts like the flu, maybe it's the flu. Or maybe it's something like the flu, another virus or virus-like microbe we've nearly all had. When I first read the theories of reactivated polio virus come alive again, either in its original form, or some genetically altered form, I was much impressed because my experience of the initial polio infection was exactly like the flu and the symptoms were back. "After the acute infection subsides, possible residual poliovirus could escape immune system surveillance as the result of antibody-induced antigen modulation, production of blocking factors, or generation of suppresser T-cells, theoretically causing persistent infection," according to Gholam H. Pezeshkpour, M.D., and Marinos C. Dalakas, M.D., in the *Arch Neurol*; vol 45: 505-507, May 1988. Inflammatory signs of leakage, lymphocytes, and other signs of infection were present. Also mentioned was the presence of dysfunction in the astrocytes, the cells which store and provide nutrients for neurons. In a follow-up study by Dalakas, "Morphologic Changes in the Muscles of Patients with Postpoliomyelitis Neuromuscular Systems," also published in 1988, *Neurology* 38:99-104, it was reported that patients treated with corticosteroids or interferon showed no response.

It was pointed out that people in both studies were excluded who had other neurologic diseases, diabetes, known exposure to toxic agents, other major viral diseases, or a family history of neurologic disease.

My question is this: did the research include specifically looking for herpes zoster, Candida or yeast acetaldehydes, and pertussis or was it only the poliovirus that was looked for?

Several things go into this question. One was an incidental analogy that was drawn between the possibility of reactivated poliovirus behaving like chickenpox in some early theories trying to account for polio reactivation. It was an analogy based on the notion that the chickenpox virus, herpes zoster, first affects many children, goes through an infectious stage, then lies dormant in the spine, sometimes never to be activated again, sometimes to become active again, but this time as shingles. The original herpes virus attacks the skin, or is believed to, resulting in blisters. Does it leave scarring and lesions on the nerve cells and the brain even though it rarely scars the skin?

Later, in a different form, normally triggered by stress, overwork, or ill health, herpes comes alive again, only to attack the nerves, usually of the lower back, or the chest, or the face. If the attack progresses into the spinal cord and the brain, it is known as meningitis. The place where herpes lies dormant in the spine is unnervingly close to the places where poliovirus is known to have done damage. And, of course, the World Health Organization is now convinced that herpes is polio. My feeling was that they were relatives, pleomorphic different generations of one another, and tricky enough to pass for the suspected but missing Epstein-Barr factor in Chronic Fatigue Syndrome, the cancer BX virus of Royal Raymond Rife, among other microbial forms, bacterial and fungal.

If relatives, is herpes a viral cousin to polio, a first generation polio parent, a third generation polio grandchild?

The Ebola Reston virus-bacteria discussed in *The New Yorker* by Richard Preston, October 26, 1992, the Ebola Zaire virus, the Marburg virus, are very suggestive of such a pedigree from something minor like chickenpox to something major like polio. All three are known to mutate rapidly from blood born viral forms, to bacterial and spore-born bacterial or yeast forms. One Hot-Zone scientist who had been watching the replication process of a virus smelled an odor coming from the corked test tube. He was on record saying that viruses never produced odors. Only bacteria did. He might have also said that yeast fermentation and mold do the same thing, but his paradigms had not accommodated the work of Royal Raymond Rife who had repeatedly demonstrated the transformation of virus to other viral forms, bacterial forms, and fungal forms. Rife knew microbes were pleomorphic, many shaped: they mutated their shapes and metabolism to survive. But the Hot-Zone scientist did not have access to his work, nor to the cautions it implied. Nor did it occur to him or Preston that the virus trapped in the test tube had found a way to get out.

It would attract a host by smell. The Hot-Zone scientist was not alarmed because the monkey virus was known to be harmless to humans. After all, the virus had been classified level two. Caution was warranted, but nothing like a space suit and multiple sterilizations were required. His fatal mistake was raising the test tube to see a scum forming in the tube. Viral activity had stopped, and a bacterial scum or mold had replaced it. He removed the cork and sniffed. It was an unusual odor that beckoned him there. Fourteen days later the scientist was dead, dead from a mutated strain that became fatal, and then mutated back again into a non-fatal form weeks later. The point of the article was to suggest that viruses mutate for a reason. Fatal viruses mutate to ensure their own survival; if they remain fatal to their hosts, they would themselves become extinct. But if they develop only nasty and annoying symptoms without destroying their host, they will be tolerated by their host. To Preston, this was a cause to celebrate.

To me, it is a cause of concern.

I believe chronic illness survivors have learned to tolerate a number of viral, fungal, and bacterial forms, all of which share the same pedigree, and all of which have slowly eaten our brains and central nervous systems. They don't eat enough to kill us; they eat only enough to survive and place us in an episodic state called chronic illness.

When I originally read about herpes-polio virus parallels, I accepted the herpes comparison as a viable analogy. Now, I wonder if the analogy is not an analogy at all, but a literal fact. If it acts like herpes, and you have a medical history of herpes zoster in chickenpox, deduction tells you part of the problem is herpes. Consider the similarities in symptoms. There is nerve pain in both instances, flu-like weakness, nerve damage, chronic fatigue. The worst of it lasts three weeks; then, you have residual fatigue for much longer. It may recur. It is episodic.

One occasion for this question was triggered by my wife getting shingles during one of my episodes of intense muscular and nerve pain. She had had no history of chickenpox. Both chickenpox and shingles are contagious. None of her teacher peers had come down with shingles or chickenpox. Did she get shingles from me? Could it be that shingles was one cause of my post polio syndrome symptoms, either aggravating the problem and/or predisposing me to them?

The most intense areas of pain that I was experiencing and have episodically reexperienced have been in the two places shingles normally attacks nerves: the chest area and the lower back area. Exactly where I saw shingles blisters on my wife's back was where I was experiencing the most pain but without skin inflammation.

My wife came home from the dermatologist with the prescription to rest and to isolate herself so the infection wouldn't spread. She was given no medication, but the brochure she was given on shingles indicated that shingles responded to pepper oil and to rest.

I had a version of pepper oil, a tea tree oil that promised to relieve the pain of shingles. I applied it daily for a week hoping it would alleviate some of the pain. For short periods of time, the pain receded.

As she lay in bed, I began reading about shingles. Here is what I found.

A chance observation by Dr. Chris Kagan at the Cedars of Lebanon Hospital, Los Angeles, noted that solutions of herpes virus cultures were always encouraged to grow with the addition of **L-arginine** to the culture. Dr. R. Tankersley found that the growth of the herpes virus in solution was considerably slowed by the addition of **L-lysine**. On the basis of these observations, a therapeutic application was attempted with excellent results. Forty-three of forty-five patients showed marked improvement when their diets were altered to avoid foods which were rich in arginine: those foods happen to be: gelatin, chocolate, carob, coconut, oats, whole-wheat and white flour, peanuts, soybeans, and wheat germ. It just so happens that our diet was rich in those foods. It was Halloween, and the trick-or-treaters had not come to our door that year. We had gorged on leftover chocolate containing large concentrations of arginine. And our diet had never been rich in foods containing a high lysine-dominant ratio: fish, chicken, beef, lamb, milk, cheese, beans, brewer's yeast, and mung bean sprouts.

We altered our diet and self medicated with L-lysine, 500 milligrams a day, a recommended dosage contained in *Amino Acids* but unknown to our dermatologist. Considering the contagious nature of shingles, I decided to take L-lysine right along with my wife. I had enough problems without adding another. At the time, I was convinced that the stress I had placed on my wife from her watching me go through my own PPS troubles were half responsible for triggering the outbreak of shingles. She was as worried about me as I was and was helpless to do anything about the pain.

I had not considered at the time that I might have actually been the viral source of the shingles in the first place. Did the intense pain I was experiencing trigger an alarm in the herpes colony in me, an alarm that said we may be killing off this host, maybe we better blast on out and try the guy's wife. Heck, she's hale and hearty. She ought to be good for a few years. I may have been the corked test tube that my wife sniffed.

For my wife, the painful part of the shingles rapidly improved after taking lysine, and she was back to work in another week. I continued taking the L-lysine because I had experienced an improved energy level and much improved ability to concentrate. A week later I got on the scales and discovered I had lost weight. I was so excited about it that I called my sister in Denver only to find that her children had come down with chickenpox. We had not seen them in over two years.

However, I had sent her a letter in the most acute phase of the pain. Every teacher knows that a paper written by a student with the flu is a dangerous thing. Teachers who wash their hands frequently during paper grading do themselves a great favor. Virus can survive and be transmitted by paper. But at the time I wrote my sister, I had not considered myself contagious.

I told her about the lysine though, and she, well, didn't believe me. But she was intrigued about the weight-loss business, sort of. So much for the credibility conferred by reading and personal experience. She didn't attempt the lysine on her children, but she tried it herself to reduce haraba thighs. Incidentally, it didn't work for her weight control. It worked just for mine.

"Other aspects of lysine's application to therapeutics include the fact that from it the body forms an amino acid called **carnitine** which is causing some interest in its role as an agent for transporting fatty acids across the mitochondria, where they can be used as a source of fuel in the generation of energy. If carnitine levels are low within the cells, then there is poor metabolism of fatty acids, thus contributing to an elevation of blood fat and triglycerides," according to Leon Chaitow, D.O., N.D., author of *Amino Acids in Therapy, A Guide to the Therapeutic Application of Protein Constituents*, 1988.

Faulty-fat metabolism has been noted in this paper before, and it was linked to lesions in the brain of PPS survivors. Perhaps herpes is the link to both, and lysine is one treatment that might rectify both. Lysine helped my pain levels and concentration; fascinatingly it had been used in Italian studies as an effective treatment for Alzheimer's.

Chaitow also notes **lysine deficiency symptoms**: reduced ability to concentrate, reduced ability to produce antibodies, chronic tiredness, fatigue, nausea, dizziness, and anemia. Interestingly, PPS and other chronic-illness symptoms parallel lysine deficiency. When we are deficient in lysine, we may invite trouble from a number of viral and neurotransmitter sources. Conversely, when we are rich in lysine, we may discourage viral activity, improve energy, and improve our mental abilities. And for some of us, we might even lose a couple of pounds.

Five hundred milligrams was noted as an average amount of lysine to try, by trial and error, as a therapeutic treatment. I experimented.

By the time the bottle ran out, my pain levels had decreased with my wife's, my energy was considerably improved, my weight went down, my concentration was better, and then I stopped using lysine. For several months afterwards, I felt pretty close to normal.

I'd like to see real study with L-lysine in all areas of chronic illness because lysine is also known to have a broad spectrum of antiviral properties at the same time it combats pain, chronic fatigue, and improves mental abilities. Lysine works by tricking a virus which requires arginine to replicate itself into thinking that lysine is arginine. The two amino acids are very similar in construction. As the lysine is taken into the virus, the virus is unable to reproduce and so becomes dormant or dies. Perhaps, no matter what the unknown bug is that may be aggravating PPS and Chronic Fatigue Syndrome, it might just respond to lysine therapy since it was noted that lysine has a broadspectrum antiviral application. It also has a generally beneficial effect on boosting metabolism and mental energy.

For similar reasons, I believed **zinc** should be a part of my intake of supplements. One M.D. found that cold and flu viruses could not reproduce themselves in an environment of zinc. I didn't want to give any virus a fair chance at nibbling away at what few nerves I had left. Dr. Richard Murray said the World Health Organization is now convinced that viral meningitis is what "polio" should have been called. If this is true, polio has not been wiped out at all. Rather than 12 cases a year, we really have 12,012 of virus caused spinal meningitis and "polio." Whatever you wish to call it, it still is causing acute infections. An antiviral diet might help a lot of people with acute infection and even more with suspected slow infection.

At one point in my search for the unknown antigen, I went to Dr. Terrence Young since he had a space-age computer diagnostic machine that apparently worked by picking up information electronically from acupuncture points. Shortly afterwards, it was classified as experimental by the AMA, and physicians are now no longer permitted to use it. Surprisingly, the machine had detected live pertussis virus in my system. Well, I'd had whooping cough as a child, and I'd later been given the DPT shots that most of us have had. It was then pointed out to me by Dr. Young, that the DPT vaccines sometimes actually caused reinfection with low level intensity that may persist for years undetected. It was another instance of slow viral infection. The only symptom I had was a persistent chronic cough that I blamed on cigarette smoking. Under periods of stress, I would begin coughing with little short coughs mixed with insucking or drawing in of the breath. Since being given a prescription remedy for pertussis, I no longer have that weird cough during periods of stress. I'd had it for years. My question is: why didn't the blood tests at the internist's office reveal the presence of pertussis? Does it not show up in the blood but only shows up in the mucous membranes of the air passages? Does it hide in the spine or brain? Has it mutated too and become a player in chronic disease states gradually draining away one's energy and health? Are there other signs in

35

the blood or elsewhere indicating an antigen presence, but it goes undetected because the bug has changed into a slightly altered form? I wonder further if this is a universal component in the medical histories of those with chronic illness, exposure to DPT vaccines, Whooping Cough itself, or both, one that all chronic-illness survivors share in common. Could pertussis account for the strange breathing and swallowing difficulties that some PPS survivors experience?

Also detected by the diagnostic machine was the presence of Candida albicans, a yeast-like fungus. According to my medical dictionary, Candida infection could take many forms affecting the mouth called oral thrush (white patches on the inner lining of the cheeks or tongue), the vagina (yeast infection), the lungs, intestines, skin, and nails (known as thrush in Britain). The medical dictionary reported that only rarely did Candida infection spread throughout the body. It is usually brought on by the use of broadspectrum antibiotics, perhaps like the 14 days of three injections per day of penicillin I received in the acute infection stage of the original polio virus. It is also brought on by poor nutrition. It is also brought on by an immune system weakened by a serious illness.

Antibiotics are known to wipe out friendly microbes in the gut at the same time they destroy unfriendly ones. Does the resulting vacuum give Candida a chance to flourish and spread? Candida is universally found in the gut. Does it stay there, or take the opportunity for a little vacation and migrate elsewhere?

As I was given caprylic acid to take care of Candida, a blood test was run to confirm or deny Candida's systemic presence. The blood test denied its systemic presence, but I had been given a specific fungicide to take care of it, Capricin, just in the event that it might be present elsewhere in the mucous membranes. Any culture taken from nearly anywhere in the body has revealed the presence of Candida. But normally it causes no problems unless it has undergone a population explosion. In "Phenolic Chemical Description," by Mark Johnson, Candida was described:

> "In the human situation it (Candida) is probably the most insidious opportunistic pathogen. It can have the capability of causing so much disruption in normal immune response as to make its presence 'invisible.'" Johnson mentions that Candida can result in a "flood of symptoms," with no "distinct pattern that applies to all."

> "Many hormones and neurotransmitters owe their provocative status to the immune disruption that occurs with yeast and subsequently disappear when yeast is under control. Additionally, diet and nutrition play a big role in food and yeast allergic patients. Some research would indicate that these people don't have undernutrition because of yeast and food allergies, but the reverse: they have yeast and food allergies because of their poor nutrition."

The poor nutrition commonality among chronic illness survivors may account, in my view, for nearly everything. Most dramatic to me was the mention of hormonal, neurotransmitter, and immune system dysfunction caused by yeast infection. Could Candida be the unknown bug responsible in whole or in part for the immune system activity noticed in biopsies of PPS survivors? Could it be the illusive microbial agent in Chronic Fatigue Syndrome? Does it always elude detection? Is this the cause of the lesions discovered by Dr. Bruno, lesions in the brain that result in neurotransmitter and hormonal disruptions?

In *The Missing Diagnosis*, by C. Orian Truss, M.D., this was precisely what was demonstrated. Every physician should read it. Every person with a chronic problem should read it for possible investigation, with the full knowledge of what symptoms are involved and what chronic illnesses have cleared up when Candida is treated.

Very competent neurologists have diagnosed the full range of neurological disorders such as multiple sclerosis in their patients. They had them. They exhibited all the symptoms.

Then by chance, they were also separately diagnosed as having chronic Candida infection, sometimes in the bowel, sometimes in other mucous membranes such as the mouth. They were then treated for Candida. Many chronic symptoms presumably unrelated to Candida disappeared in days, weeks, months, or years after treatment with nystatin for Candida. MS patients, for one, then returned to their neurologists. Fascinatingly, all symptoms of MS had evaporated. They no longer had MS.

My earlier suspicion that antibiotics, known to interrupt the bacterial ecosystem, was borne out in Candida research. Medical histories consistently confirmed two situations preceding Candida infection: a serious illness (polio infection qualifies); the use of a broad spectrum antibiotic (it was normal protocol to use penicillin during the acute phase of infection), the use of birth control pills, the use of steroidal drugs, or chemotherapy. Friendly and unfriendly bacteria are temporarily wiped out in the gut by antibiotic use, and, at the same time, the immune system is weakened. The result is that Candida flourishes. Candida is a fungoidal yeast unaffected by broad spectrum antibiotics. What happens is that Candida's competition is destroyed, so it has an opportunity to flourish and spread to other tissues via the bloodstream and by burrowing through tissue. Each time antibiotics like penicillin, erythromycin, tetracycline, or steroidal hormones such as cortisone skin preparations or birth control pills are taken, Candida has a wonderful opportunity to expand its influence. In all of these cases, the immune system can be temporarily paralyzed or rendered chronically unresponsive. The first symptom of its colonization activity is usually gas, followed by bloating, diarrhea alternating with constipation, frequently producing hemorrhoids. It is episodic in nature. I had thought it was my constitutional makeup to experience all of those things.

37

In an otherwise healthy individual, normal populations of friendly bacteria will repopulate the gut and nothing will happen to promote sickness. For many others who have had a serious illness in addition to the use of antibiotics or steroids, the yeast proliferates and mimics every other known disease state, one after another. One of the first effects is depressing the immune system further, further than that already taking place from the effects of a serious illness. Every chronic-illness symptom is written all over the Candida invasion. It can cause neurotransmitter interruptions, memory problems, inability to concentrate, clumsiness, muscular weakness, pain, insomnia, dizziness, chronic bad temper and depression in men, explosive anger and crying accompanied by depression in women, everything that PPS survivors experience. It is the most likely major player affecting chronic illness including post polio syndrome.

In "Tissue Injury Induced by Candida Albicans, Mental and Neurological Manifestations," by C. Orian Truss, M.D., published in the *Journal of Orthomolecular Psychiatry*, Truss demonstrated one clinical case after another where Candida infection was treated and other, apparently unrelated chronic diseases totally disappeared. He found exactly the same thing that Dalakas and others found in post polio biopsies of tissue: "Frequently the evidence suggests that immunologic mechanisms of tissue are involved (in Candida infection). The deposition of antigen-antibody complexes or the presence of 'autoantibodies' to one's own tissues are but two examples. The same 'dead end' is reached, however, when the search for a virus or other antigenic agent is unfruitful. The evidence indicates that an immunologic response is taking place and in some way is involved in the disease process, but the antigenic agent continues to elude discovery...By treating yeast infection and yeast allergy where found (vaginal infection, mouth infection, bowel infection, nail infection), it has been possible to demonstrate the relationship between mucous membrane infection and abnormal function in organs distant to the yeast infection and not actually themselves infected. The cases selected for presentation also demonstrate the variety of tissues that may be injured by this mechanism, as judged by the diversity of symptoms and signs that ceases when the mucous membrane infection ceased."

Dr. Truss pointed to four examples of autoimmune diseases that were placed in remission by finding and treating Candida infection: multiple sclerosis (the major autoimmune attack is on the myelin sheath of the nerve fibers), autoimmune hemolytic anemia (the major autoimmune attack is on the red blood cells), Crohn's disease (the major autoimmune attack is on the intestinal lining), systemic lupus erythematosis (the major attack is on the connective tissue of the body). As Truss pointed out, massive research has failed to come up with a cause for even one of these conditions; but chance treatment for an apparently unrelated condition resulted in improvement or total remission of these autoimmune diseases. Truss postulated that the physical link between the site of infection is yeast by-product released into the blood stream, by-products which he believes are toxic to the immune system itself. "Treatment (for Candida), by leading to a sustained reduction in the quantity of these hypothetical toxic yeast by-products, would have been responsible for normal restoration of normal suppresser mechanisms and the 'turning off' of the autoimmune attack."

Mark Johnson in "Phenolic Chemical Description" identified one of the hypothetical yeast by-products that Truss mentioned but was unable to identify as acetaldehyde, a natural product of all fermentation processes, and the most likely culprit of initiating the damage: "Acetaldehyde has a general narcotic manifestation with all the symptoms of chronic intoxication and its 'hangover' symptoms." Dr. Young explained it this way. "Candida pickles areas of your brain and nervous system. You experience hangovers and problems in thinking without having taken one drink."

In Japan, 30 documented cases have been reported. There, it is known as *meitei-sho*, drunk-disease. Candida not only produces an alcohol by-product, it also produces pure alcohol.

Dr. Carol Cooper, D.C., explained the immune dysfunction involved as the phenomenon of pseudoinfection. "In immune weakened patients, staph infections cease with antibiotic treatment. But the immune system keeps on responding to the site of the damaged tissue as if the staph germ was still present. So partially damaged tissue, really healthy tissue in a sense, continues to be attacked at the site of the original damage even though no germ is present." In other words, I said, "The original poliovirus may have pinholed the brain and spinal cord, but the 'signs of persistent infection' mentioned by doctors looking at biopsies would find absolutely nothing at the site except further damage and evidence of continuing immune activity?" Dr. Cooper said, "Exactly, except that immune system can't recognize the fact that the real virus has died. It keeps attacking healthy tissue. It's a common immune system disorder." I would say, in the instance of Candida, the aldehyde by-product, or dead yeast remnant in the bloodstream and elsewhere may just be the triggering mechanism that acts as a chemical signal that stimulates immune cell attack and invites foreign microbe interest.

I couldn't help but think this was exactly how the body responds to food allergies. Food is not a foreign invader; it's a friendly necessary substance, but the immune system in a weakened state confuses the good guys with the bad guys and suddenly all kinds of things can be irritated by a flood of senile or, I should say, aldehyde-drunken white blood cells eating the living heck out of the wrong stuff: the linings of the lungs, the nervous system, the skin, and finally the brain.

Each aspect of the Candida hypothesis satisfies the episodic nature of what I have experienced in the last three years of PPS or chronic illness. What do I mean? I was given an antifungoidal treatment for Candida, sublingual drops, and my mind slowly cleared. I was able to concentrate when I hadn't been able to before; my memory problems improved.

I had been diagnosed as having multiple food allergies. Slowly, my food sensitivities declined. I had been allergic to all but three foods: fish, oats, and eggs. Most of the rest caused extreme itching, nasal problems, and maybe ultimately part of an irritated nervous system. One of the worst was an allergy to shrimp. Eating shrimp put me into a frenzy of itching that would last for hours. But two months after fungicide had done in some of the Candida in my system, I tried shrimp again, this time with no allergic response that I was aware of. The same was true of bananas.

One common observation pointed out by Truss was that Candida is thought to be the cause of food sensitivities and allergic responses. Treatment for Candida, presumably unrelated to allergy, helped do in most of my allergic reactions. For years, I had been subject to episodic diarrhea, constipation, accompanied by enormous amounts of gas, bowel grumbling, and heartburn. These symptoms began to decline, but they did not go away. At the time I noticed these differences, I had not attributed them to the diminishment of the Candida population in my gut. I just thought my overall health was improving and my digestion went along with that. Truss does attribute improvement in digestion and something much more important to Candida infection improving: "Intestinal disease associated with chronic diarrhea may lead to vitamin and other nutritional deficiencies, which in turn may result in abnormal brain function" and a host of other physical problems which I believe become misdiagnosed. And so I experienced an episodic upswing in my symptoms for a period of months.

Then, I developed an abscessed tooth. As I was treated for that with a root canal and cap, I was also given a broad-spectrum oral antibiotic. With the antibiotic, my pain levels left the Earth's orbit. Shortly thereafter, my gum disease worsened, and I was given multiple oral surgeries, also accompanied by antibiotics, oral and topical. During those times, all of my digestive disturbances returned, and with their return, I regressed to former levels of difficulty with post polio syndrome: increased levels of pain, fatigue, insomnia. I blamed it on the discomfort of the dental work at the time.

As PPS symptoms skyrocketed, my eczema worsened: I developed acne at fifty years of age (pimples and gray hair, you got to be kidding), and I had a facial skin rash diagnosed as rosacea. Of course, I was given steroids for the eczema and more antibiotics for the skin rash. My chronic-illness symptoms dramatically worsened further.

What I did not know at the time was that skin rashes, worsening of chronic conditions, acne, digestive disturbances are directly related to the results of Candida flourishing, spreading, and raising havoc with your intestines and subsequently everything else. All I knew at the time was the over-the-counter remedy for reducing digestive disturbances: taking acidophilus capsules or acidophilus milk to repopulate your intestinal track with friendly and useful bacteria. After a bottle of acidophilus, intestinal problems diminished, and PPS symptoms declined again.

40

What I had done unwittingly was to give Candida competition. But I did not kill it. I developed white patches in my mouth and my dentist noticed them without being able to diagnose what they were. I was sent to an oral surgeon for his opinion. He could not diagnose them either, but suggested that I take notice of any growth in their size. I did not know at the time, nor did very competent doctors seem to know, that what I had in my mouth was oral thrush, yeast infection, infection brought on incidentally by the use of antibiotics. I also developed Candida infection under one fingernail and one toenail. Having learned enough from Truss and Crook to recognize Candida symptoms, I knew enough to ask for their most successful treatment from my own doctor. Candida had been back, no doubt its return accompanying the uses of antibiotics.

Not only is there a connection of Candida episodes flaring up when antibiotics are taken, it is also tied in with diet and the weather. Humid, damp, overcast weather is the perfect environment for molds to proliferate: there is a definite correlation between chronic moldy environments and the explosion of Candida infections. Candida flourishes when the weather is damp or when it is fed molds or yeasts or yeast by-products in foods. Oregon cold seasons must be the absolute worst place for people with PPS and other chronic illness and the absolute best place for Candida. Damp weather lowers the body's defenses against Candida, according to Dr. Truss.

The weather is also tied in with worsening of PPS symptoms: Candida may love moldy weather, but nerves hate it. As Dr. Bruno pointed out, gross muscular strength and coordination decline at or below 68 degrees. The barometer and the temperature may be closely linked, and a mega link is the connection with Candida population explosions.

Elements in the diet can favor the growth of Candida : "The most troublesome are the fermented beverages (especially wine and beer), aged cheeses, mushrooms, vinegar, and bread stuffs with a high yeast content."

I have routinely noticed and wondered why when I drank wine that I experienced growling, gas, and I wondered further why my favorite foods, vinaigrette salads, pizza with mushrooms, Tonic water with real sugar, always caused these problems. These foods feed the yeast; others retard its growth. And guess what I was using for a mouthwash: an alcohol-based rinse. Most mouthwashes are six percent alcohol, and I was unknowingly giving the Candida in my mouth (and possibly the seat of my gum infections) a royal snack. I couldn't help but think that the topically applied antibiotics the dentist had been swabbing on my gums was possibly exacerbating the real cause of gum disease. I have an awfully bad feeling that the pus that has never been cultured from my gums may just hide some lovely little critters who hire cheerleaders when the dentist opens my mouth, namely, Fred Fungus and his little Yeast Band. Fungal yeasts thrive on alcohol and antibiotics.

I had also mentioned to my wife that I frequently experienced a metallic taste in my mouth. "You have to be one of the most unusual people in

41

the world," she would say. Then, her eyes would roll to the ceiling, and I knew she meant "you are a hypochondriac." Not so, wife. My wife also believed that if I paid more attention, I might not drop everything I attempted to pick up. This was not true either.

I can't tolerate my wife wearing perfume, so she doesn't wear it.

Chemical intolerance to perfume, cologne, hair sprays, pesticides, furniture polish, and such things as cigarette smoke and exhaust fumes are commonplace symptoms listed in the clinical medical histories of people diagnosed as having Candida yeast infections. Metallic or salty or bad odors are sensed by those who are yeast infected. They have chronic bad tempers. I had blamed it on the PPS symptoms. I explode over stupid little things. And I wish I didn't drop every doggone thing I try to pick up. I have mechanical picker-upper arms in every room to retrieve darn near everything I touch from socks to caps on vitamin bottles, and I swear the living hair off every item I drop. Clumsiness is also a typical symptom of Candida, in my case accompanied by spontaneous and explosive combustion of the vocabulary. What I had considered eccentric Ugly Mood Swings, my UMS's, are universal in PPS survivors and may be in others experiencing chronic illness. My father had Ugly Mood Swings, and his were blamed on Alzheimer's.

It would be fascinating to know if all Candida symptoms are universal in those experiencing the post polio syndrome and other chronic conditions. I'd never brought up the metallic taste issue to a medical doctor for fear I'd be sent to the psychiatrist again. I wonder how many of those other symptoms others never bring up because they fear they are not relevant to anything. How can chronic heartburn and episodic diarrhea be relevant to anything a doctor would want to hear? In fact, I hate bringing up those things publicly and socially whether or not someone wants to hear about them.

Would you care to reveal that all of your family, mother, father, and sister are all wind instruments? But in fact, there is a genetic predisposition to yeast infections, bowel disturbances and gas.

When my acupuncturist looked at my tongue over a period of last two years and asked if I had "digestive upset," I said I didn't. I thought she was invading my privacy, reading my palm by looking at my tongue. One thing was she wasn't specific enough to get a good response from me; another thing was I didn't know enough to believe that gas and heartburn were relevant to anything. Next time she asks, I'll know what to say. But next time, I hope I won't have my digestive problem written all over my tongue.

Chapter 5

OTHER TOXINS, AMINO ACIDS, DIET, MASSAGE, AND HERBS

Dr. Frederick Maynard, M.D., a post polio survivor and physician specializing in the treatment of the post polio syndrome, highlighted his concern with environmental toxins in "Update on PPS—Research, Management and Treatment" at the Post-Polio Conference held September, 1989, in Pasco, Washington.

Although it was not clear to me why he was almost unique in PPS specialists emphasizing that care should be given to eliminating or diminishing toxins in our environment, the seminal idea seemed to come from other neurological data indicating nerve dysfunction associated with exposure to toxic agents, not necessarily connected with PPS, but pertinent to PPS in an important way. Toxic agents have been found to weaken and injure nerves in many chronic conditions: learning disabilities, anti-social behavioral problems and criminal behavior, meat-wrappers' disease, Parkinson's, Alzheimer's, Multiple Sclerosis.

The environmental hazards of the workplace where chemicals are used in the manufacturing process is well known, maybe most notoriously known through the Mad Hatter's syndrome. Workers who were close to the mercury salts used in coloring felt hat bands went literally insane. A host of toxic hazards may be present in modern manufacturing that cause countless chronic illnesses.

Another legion of toxins may be present at home. New carpeting exudes formaldehyde, as do some wood amalgams. Formaldehyde resin is used in permanent press clothing. You're breathing it when you wear it. Paints, petroleum based and acrylic, most plastics, all exude toxic gases. For many, they are the cause of debilitating allergic reactions. Styrofoam or polystyrene egg-carton toxins are absorbed through the porous surface of the eggshell into the egg. One nanogram of styrene per gram shows up in raw eggs and a host of other toxins show up in cooked eggs: the one nanogram per gram detected in a raw egg shows up as 103 nanograms per gram when the eggs are cooked. The plasticizers used in cling plastic wrap migrate into any food they touch. They have been found to debilitate meat wrappers exposed to them everyday. The ground itself exudes radon. Wool exudes pyrrole as do many plastics and synthetics. Eczema and contact dermatitis in some people is triggered by touching wool, the plastics of some pens, detergents used in washing of clothes, the use of fabric softeners, stain removers, and household cleansers. Most household products used in cleaning and polishing are considered hazardous wastes when they're

43

in the dump, according to *50 Simple Things You Can Do to Save the Earth*. Most of us don't think about them as such when they're in the home.

Fifty simple things you might do to save your nerves might involve the use of natural fabrics, the use of non-toxic household products, and the consumption of natural and uncontaminated foods.

Television and computer terminals put out low frequency radiation that is believed to be a source of stress, according to the work of John Ott and others. Positive ion emissions from such electrical devices can produce positive ion rashes. Fluorescent lights have been well-known industrial hazards for many years, not only in terms of PCBs leaking out of old ballasts, but also in terms of low X-ray emissions and the non-full spectrum nature of the light itself. Institutional studies on fluorescent lighting found that, within three hours under such conditions, irritability and aggressive behavior rise. School children become unruly. The partial spectrum of light itself destroys vitamin A in the bloodstream.

I doubt that it's possible to eliminate many of these problems. Certainly, lead-shielded full spectrum fluorescent lights exist and are marketed. Color schemes can be changed to reduce irritability: Robin's Nest Blue was found to be the most calming under fluorescent lights. Many things can be done in environmental engineering simply by changing the color scheme. Pink is used in some jails to reduce violent behavior in arrested criminals. Pink promotes calmness. Orange was found to be the absolute worst color scheme for bringing out aggressive tendencies in most people under fluorescent lighting.

Computer screens that filter out both ultra violet radiation (implicated in cataract formation) and other low-frequency radiation now exist. Wrist-rests in front of keyboards can relieve stress on shoulders. Teslar watches promise an electronic cocoon that protects a computer terminal user from excessive radiation.

Foods are frequently contaminated with pesticides that find their way into our fatty deposits and have been implicated in everything from cancer to psychosis. Feed lot animals are fed or injected a host of antibiotics, and pesticides consumed in grains are concentrated in their fat. Fish and shell-fish are frequently reported to have alarming levels of heavy metals such as lead and mercury.

The air quality in cities is frequently poor. High levels of carbon monoxide, lead, ozone, formaldehyde, and particulate matter can be toxic to lungs and nerves.

Is there any way of totally removing these things from our environment and diet?

I suspect it would be nearly impossible and highly unlikely. Electronic filters can be installed on furnaces and air conditioners to remove many of them. People have chosen to consume more organically produced foods which have no toxic contaminants and to use less toxic household products

44

and non-oil based paints. The fat in milk and in meat can be diminished. It seems that fat contains the highest concentrations of toxic by-products both in our foods and in ourselves.

What other strategies may exist?

Maybe the outside is not so easily altered, but the inside can be by massage, exercise, sweating, supplementation, and simple changes in habits.

Medicine before the turn of the century blamed most of the health problems in our bodies on toxic waste accumulating in the intestines. Skin problems were believed to be caused by the body trying to rid itself of wastes. In modern times, the British Eczema Society's homeopathic treatments suggest that skin eruptions will never improve unless toxic intakes are reduced. Less meat and more fruits and vegetables were the recommendations then and now, now by naturopaths, homeopaths, and some chiropractors. Some medical organizations promote such a practice as an anticancer and anti-heart disease preventative diet. Perhaps, it makes good common sense to alter one's diet on many levels. In fact, it's almost a consumer mega trend to manipulate your diet to include more fiber and bulk so that what fat and toxins are accumulating there may be more easily eliminated through the bowel rather than absorbed into the bloodstream through the intestinal wall. A thousand benefits of eating more fruit and vegetables are explained in *The Food Pharmacy*, by Jean Carper, a pharmacy I hope the pharmaceutical companies will promote by returning to their original interests in herbs and natural sources of healing. It would considerably reduce their costs and immeasurably improve our health if they would begin to interest themselves in natural food supplements and natural foods.

The old principle of drinking eight glasses of **water** a day to cleanse your system made good sense to medicine before the turn of the century and still makes good sense to those trying to lose weight. Flushing the system with water does move waste products through the system more easily. A slice of lemon added to the water glass is an old fashioned way of detoxifying the system, according to Dr. Khalsa. Fruit juices and vitamin C work in much the same way to detoxify, including the heavy metal toxins of mercury.

In terms of detoxifiers, **L-glutamine**, an amino acid, is a less well-known remover of toxic ammonia concentrations in the brain. Aside from being the dominant amino acid in cerebro-spinal fluid and a component of chromium glucose tolerance factor which regulates metabolism of blood sugar and energy production, Passwater points out that "The shortage of L-glutamine in the diet, or glutamic acid in the brain, results in brain damage due to excess ammonia, or a brain that can never get into 'high gear.'" It has also been pointed out that craving for alcohol and sweets diminish with the addition of L-glutamine to the diet. I suspect that such a deficiency preexisted the acute phase of polio infection, and may have in part predisposed chronic illness survivors to a susceptibility to infection. Few healthy people exposed to any virus actually get infected. Only 1% of those exposed to polio virus actually come down with the disease.

Glutamine is also a brain sugar and has been used successfully as a supplement to withdraw people from long term addictions. Could this be one of those deficiencies that go into the makeup of the PPS personality? It has been commonly observed that PPS people are addiction prone, and the surveys I circulated suggested that people were universally addicted to sweets, especially chocolate. It would be fascinating to discover if a simple amino acid deficiency, a protein deficiency, were responsible for our addictive society in general. Strangely enough, Dr. Beasley's *Betrayal of Health* noted that widespread protein deficiencies began to show up in the 1970s among other nutritional deficiencies. *The Betrayal of Health* pointed out that the first survey conducted in 48 of the United States to examine our health and nutrition status as a nation during 1971-74 (the Health and Nutrition Examination Survey, HANES) reported alarming nutritional deficiencies:

- All age categories reported vitamin A deficiencies and vitamin C deficiencies.
- Half of our women were deficient in calcium.
- Over 90% of all infants, women and children were deficient in iron no matter what their race or social status.
- The majority of American women were protein deficient, and one third of American men were protein deficient.

Toxic accumulations, vitamin, mineral, and protein deficiencies suggest much about major players in chronic illness in modern society.

In addition to exercise, sweating, vitamin C, and glutamine, **massage** does much to facilitate the body's natural detoxification process. According to Barbara Schrieber, M.A., and licensed masseuse, "Chronic tension produces chronic tightness in the musculature. The result is waste and toxic by-products of cellular activity are not moved out of the muscle cells." The hazards of marathon runners have been frequently compared to PPS symptoms in terms of an overused system that requires extended recovery time. Certainly, helping remove some of the lactic acid soreness in overused muscles makes common sense. PPS persons run a marathon every day of their lives.

Massage benefits the natural processes of the body increasing circulation. "Increased circulatory flow produces more oxygen to nourish the cells and helps get rid of those 'knots' we associate with tight necks and shoulders." In short, massage is both a natural aid to help along the body's own detoxification process and an aid in nourishing it.

The benefits extend to the lymph system of the body. The lymph system is one source of antibody activity that wards off infection and is also one of the pathways that naturally removes toxins from the body. It's recommended that you drink 4-8 glasses of water after a massage to assist in the process.

In addition, there are obvious gains from the relief of chronic pain and stress. There are benefits in flexibility and range of motion. Circulation is considerably improved.

Biofeedback studies have pointed out that a constant state of chronic stress puts the body into a state of perpetual "fight or flight." Adrenaline (epinephrine) is overproduced. Faulty emotional regulation is of particular concern to the PPS survivor, according to Dr. Richard Bruno, Physical Psychologist who specializes in the autonomic nervous system. Dr. Bruno maintains that widespread damage to the brain stem was incurred during the initial acute phase of the polio infection. One area of brain damage that he discovered involved lesions in the hypothalamus, the regulator of hormones and the stress regulator. Bruno points out that once PPS survivors react to stress, they keep on reacting. "Our body tends to react to everyday annoyances as if they are life threatening situations."

Aside from explaining my older adult personality, Dr. Bruno gives me further interest in continuing with the benefits of massage. Under continued adrenaline output, the eliminative and protective functions of the digestive and immune system are inhibited, according to massage theory. "Due to a suppressed immune and digestive system the normal functioning of the body is out of balance. We sometimes say 'We are 'run down and have caught a bug.'" And according to Hans Selye, a Montreal physician, the long term effects of stress set people up for prolonged periods of *disease* leading to real diseased conditions. Many lines of research have linked long periods of stress with all the major killers and debilitating conditions of chronic illness in modern times.

Many of the symptoms of chronic-illness syndromes are written all over the usual conditions that massage alleviates. There are two kinds of massage that I've had acquaintance with. Deep Therapeutic massage is what I've asked for and been given. Trager massage, I'm told, was specifically developed for post polio survivors. It tends to be lighter and involves more loosening motions with vibration. My one month's exposure to lighter vibrational massage produced nothing. But individuals may differ.

From my experience, Deep Therapeutic massage was wonderful to experience (not without some discomfort to be sure), but the flexibility and absence of pain following the massage have been entirely worth the minor discomfort and expense. Days to weeks of benefit have followed an hour's worth of massage depending on the season and the temperature. I found the same to be true with *Shiatsu*, Japanese acupressure, and *acupuncture* itself. They are all alternatives worth investigating as well as considerably less expensive than many conventional office visits and drug therapies.

Least expensive, of course, is doing massage yourself on the areas you can reach. Carpal tunnel syndrome was me, as were frozen shoulders and frozen pectorals. Those areas I can reach, and I can reach them with some benefit with a daily soap-assisted massage in the bath. When the pains become more intense, *Aloe Ice*, an anti-inflammatory and muscle relaxant gel, which includes witch hazel, aloe vera gel, menthol, cinnamon oil, tea tree oil, potassium chloride, lithium chloride, has been a life-saving, sleep-saving, money-saving addition to my life. So has *Zheng Gu Shui*, a Chinese over-the-counter remedy for muscle pain. Eat an apple and steal a ruble from the doctor. Massage yourself with a natural anti-inflammatory muscle relaxant and steal a treatment expense from your chiropractor and your masseuse. Or read a book on home massage and get a friend or spouse to do it. You won't be sorry. There is a kind of magic healing in the human touch that has been known and practiced as long the expression "laying on of hands" has been in existence.

Some physicians refer patients to massage therapists for: headaches, anxiety, depression, arthritis, and insomnia. Most of those conditions are associated with PPS and other related chronic illness.

The other major eliminative organ of the body mentioned in old medical texts is the lungs. Modern living seems to encourage rapid shallow breathing. Old remedies for chronic conditions always included fresh air and sunshine. Modern relaxation techniques and pain management techniques ask the person to not only slow down during the day, but take time out to breathe, slowly and deeply for a few minutes. It strengthens the stomach muscles and thereby lessens stress on your back.

One benefit is that **full deep breathing** slows your heart rate (it does) and expels toxins from your blood. It's a common biofeedback relaxation technique. And if Edgar Cayce was right, deep breathing changes overly acidic conditions of the blood back to healthy normal. And, of course, deep breathing doesn't cost anything to try except for time and effort.

One pain management technique involves breathing into an area of tension or pain, then imagining the tension releasing and the pain departing out of that area. I learned it in Dr. Khalsa's office. You might want to try it. It works.

Ginseng has been around from at least 2000 B.C. It has been used by billions of people as a preventative and treatment to restore strength and vigor and to 'stay young,' despite modern American pharmaceutical companies' inability to discover what's in it or why it works, according to Barbara Krieg in *The Search for Plants that Heal, Green Medicine,* a history of pharmaceutical research. It's called panax quinquefolium or panax Schinseng; panax or panacea, good for everything; and Jin-Chen, the Chinese word for manlike because of the shape of the root, a whole body with head, arms, and legs. *Green Medicine* history states only that American drug companies have had a "marked absence of interest in ginseng." Krieg mentions that preliminary chemical testing in Germany and Holland claimed only to discover unknown inert substances. She said that the feeling seems to be in most of the United States and Europe that "cure alls cure nothing." She failed to mention that if such an inexpensive substance did work that billions in revenue could be jeopardized. Of course, they'd make it back if they sold ginseng and found better ways to farm it. It normally grows only in the wild, and is paradoxically prone to many diseases. It is a frail plant that promises great strength.

Despite her industrial spokesperson role, Krieg tried the herb herself and mentions in a footnote that on days when she took the herb that "Over a period of weeks, I consumed a precious root doll (of ginseng) in tiny nibbles. On the days I had ginseng, I seemed to have very vivid, complex dreams at night...A Stanford University neurophysiologist suggests that dreams may have a chemical basis, being initiated by the body's efforts to rid the central nervous system of some naturally created poison. Could it be that ginseng achieves its results by augmenting this process?" My experience of vivid, complicated, intricate dreams has been the same over a period of two months taking the herb everyday. I've noticed that the character of the dreams has changed from something nightmarish to something very pleasant though. The complexity and vividness continue, however, as do slowly increasing levels of energy.

Jean Carper's *The Food Pharmacy, Dramatic New Evidence That Food is Your Best Medicine* mentioned the Doctrine of Signatures and its application to ginseng. It was a theory that showed medical texts from the seventh century B.C. using the Doctrine to choose remedies in ancient Assyro-Babylonia. "Its simplicity is appealing. The idea is that for every part of the human body there is a corresponding part in the world of nature. That concept flows from the ancient belief that man's 'little world,' or microcosm, is a direct reflection of the 'larger world,' or macrocosm. Thus, in nature you will find a counterpart for every bit of human anatomy." She goes on to say that traditional Chinese medicine's ginseng became known as a "whole body tonic," a source of vitality and long life, because the root itself resembled the whole human body.

Apparently escaping the attention of the old wise ones was the resemblance of the central nervous system with all plants and trees: at a mineral level, fruits and vegetables all serve the maintenance and health of nerves and the brain. The Greek word *dendrites* fascinatingly to me means tree-youth, and is the etymological origin of the modern anatomical term describing the branches of the nerves and neurons.

Although the Western and European world has expressed little interest in its research, ginseng was the object of more than 400 studies in Russia. "Repeatedly, they affirmed that people drinking ginseng tea appear generally healthier, feel better, withstand stress better, have more energy and concentrate better," according to Carper.

Dr. Farnsworth has theorized that ginseng functions as an "adaptogen," a concept defined by the Russian physician Dr. I. I. Brekhman, a member of the former U.S.S.R. Academy of Sciences. "An adaptogen is said to be a harmless substance that possesses a normalizing function. It tends to right whatever is wrong with the body. If your blood pressure is too high, it brings it down; if too low, it brings it up." Aside from having a broad spectrum of effects, it was found to be a powerful antioxidant, a free radical scavenger, and protector against toxic chemical cross linking, which in part accounts for the aging of cells and the presence of lipofusen, aging pigmentation on the skin, the nervous system, and the brain.

One study claimed that it literally regrew brain tissue, and Dr. Asai in Japan found its germanium mineral component to touch every cell of the body within 24 hours, manipulating cellular oxygen, reducing tumor growth, and assisting prescription medication to do its intended purpose with fewer side effects. Albert Y. Leung, *Chinese Herbal Remedies* (1984) mentioned more of the Japanese and Russian findings: in addition to ginseng being found to have a B-vitamin complex and multiminerals, it was also found to contain vegetable steroids, (sitosterol was the one identified), an unidentified volatile oil, and numerous saponins (foam-forming glycocides called panaxocide and ginsengocide were among them). According to Leung, the saponins are responsible for ginseng's magical effects in detoxification, raising general vitality, improving strength, calming nerves, reversing some of the effects of aging, and scavenging for free radicals that can damage organs and tissues.

Vitamin E, aside from helping to maintain and protect the central nervous system, is also known to be a free-radical scavenger protecting against injury to the cells.

My own experience of ginseng has been a significant increase in vitality gradually growing over a period of months: my general ability to do things and my peace of mind. For something that promises so much, it may be worth your looking into it. If it is purchased at a healthfood store where it's available in bulk, it is quite inexpensive to fill your own capsules. It is taken in many forms from capsules to tea.

According to my acupuncturist, Margorie Eng, Licensed A.C., ginseng is "herbal acupuncture." Like the adaptogen explanation of Dr. Brekhman, she says that it has a homeostatic effect like acupuncture itself: it tranquilizes and calms what needs to be; it stimulates what needs to be stimulated. It has a balancing function.

Jethro Kloss, an herbalist physician with forty years of experience, has this to say about ginseng. "It has been used successfully to treat and prevent all manner of illness, useful in digestive disturbances, treats chest troubles and reduces inflammation."

Part of my interest in ginseng was to explore the effects of a very old herbal treatment, and my second interest was to remove **mercury** and other possible toxins from my system. In doing research for a novel several years ago, I became interested in the behavioral effects of mercury poisons which included chronic fatigue, tremors, fasciculations, especially of the facial muscles, depression, insomnia and more bizarre things. Some speculation in the research I read was given to mercury amalgam fillings, known as silver fillings, and many chronic complaints that seemed to disappear after having the fillings removed.

Dr. Hal Huggins, *It's All in Your Head,* reported that of 30 Multiple Sclerosis patients, all 30 were off crutches and out of wheelchairs shortly following removal. A mentally ill patient was no longer mentally ill six days after removal. John Ely, Ph.D., reported that people with long-term food allergies either have allergies disappear or diminish, Candida infections subside or disappear, and immune system functions return to normal. In reverse, those having as few as 9 small amalgams placed in their mouths experienced the onset of "slow-brain." Joyal Taylor, *A Consumer's Guide to Dental Fillings,* mentioned that mercury inhibits acetylcholine, which is partly responsible for proper muscular contraction, mental concentration, and good memory. That was plenty to suggest to me that toxin removal was worth looking into.

For one thing, there was something called "Sudden Remission" from mercury-induced chronic illness that followed an episode of **sweating**, whether caused by a sweat bath or exercise. Those rare times I did sweat, I swear I did experience something like sudden remission of all my troubles. I wanted more.

Okay, I wanted to try having my fillings removed to see if it would help me. One of the major contentions in the mercury literature is that mercury is severely toxic to normal nerves. I believed I had damaged nerves, and I wanted to clean up my internal environment as best I could.

My dentist was not sympathetic. He gave me a number of authority-trouncing horse laughs before he stopped to say: "I'm not worried about mercury amalgam fillings for my patients at all. But I am worried about it for myself."

"Why are you worried about it for yourself?"

"I'm exposed to it everyday," he said.

I believe he is right to be concerned, and the rest of the dental profession might justifiably take precautions considering that autopsies show dentists to have 500% more mercury in their brains than their patients. And too, since Alzheimer's autopsies normally show the same percentage of mercury toxicity as our good dentists, there is cause to be concerned. What's more, if patients have but only one filling in their teeth, they too are exposed to it everyday. It's-all-in-your-head is the physical location of fillings. But mercury doesn't stay in the fillings long. Within twenty-four hours, Christopher Malmstrom, D.D.S., found a 3000 fold increase in the level of mercury in the fecal matter of an 11-year-old Swedish girl who had never had a mercury filling before. Joyal Taylor, D.D.S., in a *Consumer's Guide to Dental Fillings,* found that gum chewing multiples the amount of mercury in your blood 6 to 15 times. Even sheep have proved that it's not all in our heads. They were chosen because they constantly chew, and it didn't take long for mercury to wind up in the rest of their tissues even though they did not chew gum, only grass.

Dr. Taylor found that mercury causes muscle twitching and irregular heartbeats because it inactivates **acetylcholine**. The acetylcholine connection might just explain why people with mercury fillings have bad short-term memories: acetylcholine is partly responsible for good memory and concentration as well as proper muscle functioning. It also helps explain why Alzheimer's patients, when autopsied, show 5 to 8 times the amount of mercury in their brains as people who stay healthy. It should be pointed out for the inspiration of dentists who expose themselves and their patients that dentists show the same levels of mercury poisoning as Alzheimer's patients.

I've never been able to decide whether my dentist is a comedian, a contrarian, or a survivor of mercury poisoning. Perhaps his own exposure to mercury accounts for certain bizarre patterns in his thinking. I don't know. But I did decide to honor his point of view. I honored it for three years; then, I decided it was time to honor my own point of view. I wanted the fillings out, and if he wouldn't do it, then I'd go elsewhere.

He took them out, two at a time, over a period of one year. I noticed no changes in any symptoms during the time of removal. Then, about two weeks after the last mercury amalgam was gone from my mouth, but not necessarily my system, I began to notice less headaches, a more relaxed neck, and much less painful shoulders—all the time.

In my next six-month visit, I told him what was happening. He said it was all in my head. (Well, that was where the fillings used to be.) He said it must have been a placebo effect. I said placebo effects last no longer than two weeks. He said where did you read that. I told him I read it from a chemist's research, Durk Pearson's. He didn't believe me and of course hadn't read that book.

Then, I said I thought that there was a possible connection between the prior location of the fillings and the areas on my body that seemed to be experiencing much less pain.

My dentist said, "There is absolutely no evidence to suggest that the head is connected with the body."

I didn't draw him a picture, but he may be the only organism on this planet who thinks that.

Chapter 6

BRAIN CHEMISTRY AND AMINO ACIDS

I was encouraged when I found out that Dr. Lewis Krakauer, M.D. and PPS survivor, believed the same way I did. He thought that PPS, Parkinson's, Alzheimer's, Multiple Sclerosis were related. Had he included Lupus, Fibromyalgia, Chronic Fatigue Syndrome, and Psychosomatic Chronic Illness generally we would have been in total agreement. He believed that supplying one remedy, Eldepryl or Deprenyl, normally given as the last drug of choice for Parkinson's would work for all three conditions, provided the dosage was cut down. He first tried it on himself, and then found more and more willing to join his study. Eldepryl worked by supplying dopamine to the brain. For him, it was a great success. And I still hope for great things with his studies of Eldepryl and its effect on brain chemistry. I wish him and all others total success with his approach. Eldepryl is expensive, from $4 to $2 a pill, but for many it may just do the job.

However, I am wary of drug therapies for several reasons. As they help one thing, they sometimes make another worse. There are many possible toxic side effects and toxic interactions with common foods. In Parkinson's research, Eldepryl sometimes helped, sometimes exaggerated symptoms like fatigue and depression. In my own experience, I'd taken the typical vaccines, routinely been given antibiotics for ear and other infections, and I'd had three shots of penicillin per day for 14 days during the acute phase of my initial polio infection. I've wondered how many other people subject to chronic illness have been exposed to the routine use of antibiotics, vaccines, and other drug therapies. Penicillin did little to alter the course of my polio infection, but it may have done much to weaken my immune system and provide an environment where Candida would thrive. A commonplace observation in England by the British Eczema society is that eczema patients had been, past tense, routinely treated with steroidal preparations frequently combined with antibiotics. Having been subject to eczema myself after the onset of PPS, I was given prescription strength hydrocortisone treatments to apply topically, and antibiotics for a number of skin rashes.

What I didn't know, since it isn't popular in this country to know, is that steroidal and antibacterial preparations make skin conditions worse over a period of time. The immune system is weakened more and more. At least, that's the contention of the British physicians who successfully treat eczema after the long term effects of the other drugs wear off or work themselves out of the system. It was also my experience: antibiotics and steroids worsened pain and muscle twitchings.

I suspect my immune system may have been compromised by the use of penicillin and other antibiotics and so my reasons for not being enthusiastic about my own participation in drug therapies. They may have also set up a condition where Candida underwent massive colonization. In an article about the benefits of massage and naturally derived antibiotics, I found a contention that supported one of my misgivings: "Naturally derived antibiotics stimulate the body's own defense system without causing adverse effects...For example, phenol is a strong antibacterial substance found in thyme and lemon. Pure phenol, however, will not only destroy bacteria, but will also destroy healthy human tissue." As it was pointed out that natural immune boosters work more slowly, Jean Valnet also said, "Their efficacy in destroying microbes is matched only by their harmlessness to tissue." Prescription antibiotics don't improve the body's own immune system functioning; they take the place of what the immune system generally does.

After 42 shots of penicillin, I had one more for acute bronchitis a year later. I broke out in the most impressive strawberry field of hives on record. Yet when I ate blue cheese, which has one natural strain of penicillin in it, I had no allergic reaction.

So my feelings were to explore natural means of accomplishing similar things that drug therapies promised: vitamins, minerals, mineral salts, and naturally occurring amino acids in both food and supplement form all held the same promise, working by strengthening the system, not by replacing natural functions.

Peruvian Bark, Cinchona officinalis is non-toxic, but the extract quinine can be in large doses. Those things that are not believed to be toxic were where my interests lay. Enough that was toxic has happened to my nervous system.

I took some inspiration from the notations in PPS research which compared paralytic polio to normal aging and even those that compared it to accelerated aging. A kind of accelerated aging seemed to me an exact description of most chronic illness. Perhaps, accelerated-aging observations contained other clues. It was mentioned that a 65 year old typically has lost 20 percent of his or her neurons by that age. It was also pointed out that a person with one limb paralyzed has lost about the same number of nerves: 20% of your body is nonfunctional and 20% of the axons have been destroyed.

Translation: at 13 years of age, I was neurologically speaking, an old man. I was called one. The child in me died an early death, and I walked like an old person. When I started complaining about fatigue and pain and weakness to my boss in later adult life, he simply said "you're growing old." Indeed, I was, but at a slightly more advanced rate than my years

54

would suggest. If I was 65 at 13, what was I at 50? I didn't want to think about it, or the further loss of nerve integrity that must resemble very, very old age. Treatments which promised to return the brain and nervous systems to more youthful levels were very appealing to me.

Dr. Krakauer was working with a drug therapy that might resupply the brain with old age deficiencies in dopamine-related neurotransmitters. Amino acids can do the same kind of thing in a natural and non-toxic way. His inspiration came in part from a discussion with a neurologist unfamiliar with PPS syndrome, but who had noticed that the PPS symptoms that Dr. Krakauer was describing resembled other nerve disorders where the addition of neurotransmitters had proved helpful.

My inspiration came from an observation made by Burk Jubelt, M.D., in a 1987 *Accent On Living* interview. "...the muscle cannot get adequate 'nourishment' or nutritional support from the nerves...the problem occurs because the nerves aren't providing the appropriate signals to the muscle," according to Dr. Jubelt. In the *Archives of Neurology* in June 1988, "Functional Recovery, a Major Risk Factor for the Development of Post Poliomyelitis Muscular Atrophy," by Jeffrey Klingman, M.D., and others, it was pointed out: "The maintenance of extended motor units imposed increased metabolic demands on both the motor neurons and the sarcomeres and may conceivably predispose to premature dysfunction and cell death."

The obvious implication to me was to feed the increased metabolic demands, to provide extra nourishment for overworked nerves that need it. And that included nutrition for the brain where neurotransmitters are normally produced.

In fact, normal aging may take more of a toll on the brain than it does on the spinal cord. The brain cells use neurotransmitters to communicate with each other. In youth, brain cells manufacture all of what is needed to carry on learning, remembering, moving the muscles, sleeping, and normal emotions. "As your brain ages, the ability of your brain to make and respond to some of these vital messenger chemicals drops off. In some cases, we can increase the amounts of the deficient neurotransmitters, thus bringing function in aging brains up to young or near young adult levels.

"Neurotransmitters are made by the brain from nutrient substances you eat in your food. For example, **acetylcholine** is a neurotransmitter which is important in the parts of the brain affecting primitive emotions like sex and the degree of responsiveness to outside stimuli (as in alertness versus sleep), and also plays a very important role in memory, learning, and long-term planning," according to Durk Pearson and Sandy Shaw in *Life Extension, a Practical Scientific Approach*, 1982.

Considering that Dr. Bruno had pointed out that the sleep-wake mechanism has been damaged in the hypothalamus of PPS survivors, and it is the common experience of many with PPS that they have sleep disturbances, it seemed important to me to find out if a kind of non-drug alternative nutritional supplementation could make a difference not only for the emotional benefits of a "good night's sleep" but for the body's own sense of healing itself when it has adequate rest.

"There are patterns of chemical changes that occur in the brain and body during sleep. One especially important biochemical rhythm is the release of growth hormone (GH) shortly after sleep begins. Adequate GH is necessary for proper function of the thymus and its 'troops,' the T-cell immune system that defends the body against bacteria, atherosclerotic plaques, viruses and cancer, and autoimmune self-attacks such as rheumatoid arthritis. If sleep is delayed or interrupted, a GH release can be eliminated, reduced, or aborted.

"...The cholinergic nervous system in the brain is what controls body movement and sensory sensitivity during sleep. Too much or too little can cause excessive motor activity, such as sleepwalking or endless tossing and turning. In aged persons, there is a sharp decline in activity of the cholinergic system which leads to faulty sleep, particularly involving restlessness and frequent awakening not caused by urinary urgency."

In fact, restlessness of muscles during the time a person wishes to sleep is a minor variation of sleepwalking: signals to the muscles continue to be sent when they shouldn't be. Feeding extra nutrients to the cholinergic system helps regulate this sleep dysfunction. **Choline**, a B vitamin, as a nutrient is converted to acetylcholine in the brain. Acetylcholine levels help regulate normal sleep AND normal wakefulness. Two paradoxical effects happen: the increased acetylcholine levels assist in undisturbed sleep at night and, during the day, improve memory and the ability to concentrate. "In addition, too low acetylcholine levels cannot support normal motor (muscular activity) control, and coordination and motor response falter," according to Pearson.

It seems as simple as one, two, three. The faulty sleep patterns, the faulty mentation patterns, and the muscular weakness patterns in post polio syndrome and many other neuromuscular diseases may all be connected to a deficiency of one B vitamin in the diet. With the increased demands of overworked nerve units, it seems no wonder we have problems in three related areas.

There may be a fourth connection. From a different psychiatric point of view, various methods were attempted to control anxiety and what is now called muscular tension and stress by chemical means. Kathe and Walter Misch, in 1932, found that by using intramuscular injections of acetylcholine, they succeeded in counteracting the anxiety states of their patients. When muscles were injected with acetylcholine, the patients relaxed and regained normal muscle tone. Many things may argue for tense muscles in PPS survivors: overfiring muscular neurons, simple overuse, and unresolved stress connected with the reoccurrence of polio symptoms. With the simple addition of choline, "the choline reaction appeared identical with the body's response in a state of pleasurable relaxation." The reverse was noted when adrenaline was injected, one of the chemical causes of 'fight or flight' response, tense and painful muscles.

This fourth connection may involve the dysfunction of the stress-regulator response. Choline supplementation promises to improve four conditions: faulty stress regulation, faulty sleep patterns, faulty muscular activity, and faulty memory and concentration. One B vitamin deficiency may set us up for all stress-related illness; one B vitamin sufficiency may strengthen and rejuvenate us in many ways.

As Pearson and Shaw maintain, the cholinergic system can be partly restored by extra supplementation of lecithin, or its component parts, inositol and choline, available in vitamin form, frequently included in B complex stress formulas, or available as a food supplement at health food stores as a food. All the B vitamins are important for maintaining the central nervous system. Some list **inositol** as a B vitamin, calling it a muscle sugar on the one hand and a sleep facilitator on the other.

As Dr. Chaitow has pointed out, "The ability of the brain neurons to manufacture and utilize a number of neurotransmitters...acetylcholine...is dependent upon the concentration of both amino acids and choline in the bloodstream." With all of the benefits in sleep that are potentially promised by taking a supplement, I couldn't resist adding choline and inositol to my diet. My diet had never included much fish, blackstrap molasses or brewer's yeast, which are the usual food sources of choline.

My experience has been and is that choline-inositol or lecithin supplementation did in fact help me get to sleep, stay asleep, and get a restful sleep with all the benefits of GH production that come from undisturbed rest. As has been often observed, PPS symptoms respond to undisturbed sleep. All illness responds to undisturbed sleep which allows the natural repair mechanisms of the body to work. The trick to me was getting undisturbed rest. Choline supplements seem to me a useful lifetime strategy for managing four symptoms.

Another factor beyond faulty sleep-wake regulation is pain. On many occasions, I may have had no problem with my sleep-wake regulator at all after adding choline to my nutrition. I felt no pain while asleep. The regulator itself was small potatoes alongside of intense stabbing pain in my chest, my shoulders, and numbing dull pain in my lower back. No matter what way I turned, stood, sat, or lay down, I couldn't find a comfortable position. The slightest movement produced a new knifing jab. I tried different positions, cushioning with pillows, twelve aspirin a day, or Tylenol 3, or eight Advil without success. I was considerably depressed at the same time. High levels of pain and depression seemed to be co-partners. The weather was cold and damp, and I had just begun taking allergy shots. As Jethro Kloss had pointed out to me, nerve irritation and pain can be CAUSED by cold-damp climate. I couldn't do anything about that.

I went for a month of vibrational massage and chiropractic from an M.D. who had credentials in many areas: chiropractic, acupuncture,

57

naturopathy, homeopathy, and medicine. During the acute phase of pain, the treatments, including stretching, seemed to make things worse. I was advised to use heat, and I did without success. Each allergy shot was followed by muscles turning into knots of writhing snakes.

My wife and sister said to reverse my strategies. I couldn't change the weather, but I could try something different than I was presently trying. I used heat and cold alternately, as Jethro Kloss had suggested for relieving nerve irritation. That gave temporary relief. I had recently started to take allergy shots, and I discontinued them. I was partly convinced that they were making things worse. I felt the allergy shots may have been a triggering mechanism since they work homeopathically, that is they can literally put your body in a crisis reaction before it can get better. Part of the crisis reaction can be irritating nerves, lungs, and skin. One hour after taking the first shot, I was as weak as the original acute polio infection stage, started coughing, couldn't breathe, and was in pain, world-class, everywhere. The homeopathic hair of the dog that bit me had grown into a monster gobbling me up. Well, with crisis-reaction cures like those, I wanted chronic levels of the disease back. To hell with that cure. It was much worse than the disease. And yet, and yet, there is an important connection suggested by my chance experience. Allergic reactions themselves could easily account for all post polio problems, all problems with chronic pain, chronic fatigue, weakness. I don't think they are the cause, however, but a sign of another related problem—Candida infection.

I must say one good thing about those shots that I continued for a month. A chronic cough from sinus congestion went away and has never returned. Beyond that though, allergy shots are for other people, not me. Food rotation is, though. That, I can handle. If you know you are allergic to a food, you can avoid it as a routine part of your diet. Never eat the same food several days in a row. If you eat such an allergy producing food only rarely, you may not even have an allergic reaction.

I decided to try something more natural. Pain killers didn't work, maybe something that encouraged the body's own pain killers would. And another amino acid does exactly what I wanted: **D and L phenylalanine**. At that time, my two world class complaints were: pain and depression. D-L phenylalanine helped do in both.

"The form of phenylalanine found in the animal protein diet of man is laevo, or left handed phenylalanine. That found in plant and bacterial cultures is dextro, or right-handed phenylalanine. ... There also exists a racemic mixture consisting of equal parts of d- and l- forms, which is known as DL-phenylalanine, or more simply DLPA. The original study reporting the pain controlling aspect of DLPA was published in 1978, by Dr. Seymour Ehrenpreis and colleagues of the University of Chicago Medical School...Patients were selected on the basis that other forms of treatment had failed (to produce pain relief). Pain relief in a variety of conditions, ranging from whiplash injury to osteo- and rheumatoid

58

arthritis, was rapid and lasting. There were no adverse side effects noted, nor was there any degree of tolerance, i.e., the pain relief did not diminish with subsequent use. Pain relief took from one week to four weeks to reach its optimum level, and frequently lasted for up to a month after the cessation of treatment," as reported by Dr. Chaitow in *Amino Acids in Therapy.*

Phenylalanine inhibits enzymes responsible for the breakdown of the body's own pain-killers, endorphins and enkephalins. "This appears to allow the pain relieving attributes of endorphins a longer time span for their pain relieving action." Phenylalanine is not an analgesic like aspirin, but allows "the endogenous pain control mechanism of the body to act in a more advantageous manner."

Chaitow noted that "patients with chronic pain problems have reduced levels of endorphin activity in the cerebrospinal fluid and serum" and that addition of DLPA as a supplement enhanced the restoration of the body's own pain control mechanism to its normal levels. One amino acid deficiency, DLPA deficiency, may just be a player in the pain levels that accompany chronic illness.

One hundred to 500 mg were the standard dosage, with caution to individuals with hypertension and phenylketonuria (PKU). Neither individual should attempt DLPA, nor should anyone taking an MAO inhibitor (the combination can produce extremely high blood pressure), nor with preexisting melanoma. DLPA can raise blood pressure, but normally does not with a nutritious diet and low levels of dosage. It was also recommended that after pain relief is experienced, dosage should be lowered, and finally eliminated. In some human and animal studies reported by the *Well Mind Association,* lower doses were more effective generally. A standard dosage might be 500 mg, but 250 mg actually may work better for most individuals.

When pain levels begin to return, clinical studies suggest one week of taking DLPA should be sufficient to restore adequate levels in the system.

Considerably more dramatic was the disappearance of depression in my experience of taking DLPA. It took one month for the DLPA to have an effect on my pain, but it took only two days for my depression to evaporate. The emotional cloud I was living under scattered pretty damn quick. Chaitow, Pearson and Shaw have also noted the "antidepressant" effect 24 hours to 48 hours after taking DLPA. Phenylalanine is not only an inhibitor of enzymes that break down the body's pain control mechanisms, it is a precursor to a number of neurotransmitters that facilitate memory, forestall mental fatigue, and loss of concentration, norepinephrine or NE being the chief neurotransmitter responsible for gains in mental alertness and an antidepressant effect. Pearson and Shaw point out that vitamins C and B6 are required to convert the nutrient amino acid DLPA into NE. Many over-the-counter preparations include the supporting vitamin nutrients.

59

Of the many things that phenylalanine is a precursor to are: tyrosine which is a precursor to thyroid, adrenocortical hormones, dopa, and dopamine, finally norepinephrine. High levels of dopa and dopamine are neurotransmitters associated with a proper functioning hypothalamus. Deficiency of dopamine is associated with sleep disorders. In addition, deficiency symptoms include low body temperature and restless legs. All deficiency symptoms are implicated in PPS, Parkinson's, Alzheimer's, and chronic syndromes generally.

Chaitow also points out that the use of amino acids like either tyrosine or DLPA are other ways of achieving what MAO treatments for Parkinson's disease have attempted. DLPA is a less expensive alternative to Eldepryl and other similar medications. Also, to increase brain levels of serotonin and norepinephrine, tyrosine and tryptophan have been used together with some success. It was noted too that small doses have been not only more effective than large doses, but also have fewer side effects and toxic reactions. I had better results with 250 mg than with 500 mg, for example.

Although Chaitow did not emphasize any usual side effects of DLPA in itself when combined with a normal diet, Pearson and Shaw issued a very strong warning: prescription-drug MAO inhibitors should never be combined with DLPA. Extremely high blood pressure can result. Also interestingly, should you put too much DLPA in your system, irritability and insomnia can take place as well. The lowest possible effective dose may be a handy rule of thumb for amino acids or anything else. And too, a supplement that you don't have to take all the time may be as appealing to your personality as to your pocket book. It was to mine.

The same may be true of vitamin and mineral supplements. You may not need them all the time. **Niacin**, or vitamin B3 is taken by some individuals as a sleep aid. Benzodiazepine receptors are stimulated by niacin, and when taken during the day niacin frequently causes flushing, itching, and drowsiness. The drowsiness effect can be used to one's advantage as a sleep aid, as can **inositol**, which works on the same receptors, taurine, and GABA (GABA induces calmness and tranquillity and has been shown to have a positive effect on prostate disorders, that, for some men, are responsible for sleep disturbances because of pressure causing urinary urgency).

Tryptophan which I had also used with great success as a sleep aid is now unfortunately no longer on the market. It seems that the pharmaceutical company lobbies have exerted increasing influence against natural supplementation. Anyway, bananas, turkey, and warm milk are still on the market and work the same way as the supplement.

At the beginning of this discussion, I alleged that PPS survivors and others subject to chronic illness may have much more in common than first meets the eye. I borrowed the description of an overachieving Type-A personality from an acupuncture book concerning an imbalance in the liver meridian: the function of the liver meridian was said to store nutrients and energy for physical activity, cultivating resistance against disease, and supplying, analyzing and detoxifying blood to maintain physical energy. An imbalance in the liver meridian may account for all the symptoms that set us up for chronic illness: nutrient deficiencies, toxic excesses, lowered resistance to all diseases, overuse, overwork, overdoing everything, all go together.

On general principles, I take periodic **acupuncture** treatments. It is said that acupuncture was partly discovered through war injuries just as most of modern science has advanced during discoveries made from soldiers damaged in war. In acupuncture, it was observed that arrow wounds were sometimes accompanied by the disappearance of lifetime chronic conditions. The information was slowly recorded and expanded by experimentation. For the antiquity of the knowledge, the wealth of the tradition, and the promise of its benefits, it is well worth inquiry. There are Chinese herbal remedies for each symptom discussed in this book.

I can work a full day at home, where I can rest in between work sessions, pace myself, and take a nap. It's a very different way of living. I've come to think of it as a privilege and an opportunity to put together some of the things I've learned. When I've tried to return to my overdoing-it lifestyle, I get into trouble with pain and everything else. Out come the amino acids and the sleep aids. When I pay attention to a slower life style, I need very little beyond good nutrition and adequate rest, 10 to 11 hours a day. In an important sense, I've changed my personality. I'm no longer the person hell-bent on working until exhausted. On the other hand, I believe I've taken on and understood much of the constellation of what the major players are in chronic illness and what you can do about it. Only a modified Type-A would do that.

Chapter 7

COENZYME Q10 AND CELL SALTS

- How Q10, ATP, and muscle strength are related
- Pacing yourself and me
- Q10 and deficiencies: weak muscles, shaky movements, irritability, and fatigue
- Q10 and chronic illness symptoms
- Q10, manganese, selenium, and vitamin E
- Q10 in food sources
- Q10 in muscle building programs and skin renewal
- Q10 in Japan
- Q10 and European and Japanese therapies
- Q10 promotes life extension with health and vigor in mice
- Q10 and doubling antibody production in mice
- Q10 and immune-system health related to the absence of childhood illnesses
- Scars left on the immune system by childhood illnesses
- PPS's Swiss-cheesed brain, Swiss-cheesed Creutzfeldt-Jakob, and CFS
- T-suppresser cells and immune disorders are linked
- Q10 and harmful fatty acids; vitamins A, C, E to prevent further injury
- Ginseng and Q10
- Q10 by fresh juicing your fruits and vegetables
- Q10 and Multiple Sclerosis remission
- Q10 and me: improvements in strength and endurance within one week of taking 10 mg of Q10
- Q10 assists drug therapies
- A request for clinical, self-help, and laboratory studies in the U.S. on Q10
- A personal stretching exercise program: the Johnny-Carson turkey chest
- How homeopathic *Nerve Tonic* helps cold feet and most chronic illness symptoms
- My disclaimer about using this information and my hope that it will work
- My hope for combining all levels and branches of health care with informed patients, all branches of medicine and medical science, and all professional branches of health care: a new task force approach

- The corruption of information that patients and professionals are subject to when information is filtered through the system from scientist to corporate salesman to doctor, and from doctor to patient

At one point in looking for answers, I ran across a post polio study that investigated the chemical effects of exertion within the muscles. Small amounts of exertion were found to rapidly decrease strength and increase the necessity for recovery time. ATP (adenosine triphosphate) levels associated with strength were found to be quickly depleted with small amounts of exertion. The study suggested that pacing and rest were warranted in PPS survivors to allow for recovery of ATP "energy carriers" which in turn facilitate muscular strength.

The study bore out the usefulness of the extra-rest coping strategies suggested elsewhere. Extra rest is a common sense way of dealing with any illness especially one involving weakness. But could there be other ways of enhancing some of the ATP levels to assist in this process? Why was it that ATP levels were quickly depleted in the first place? What are some of the symptoms of the ATP cycle not functioning properly?

Faulty functioning of ATP (part of the citric acid or Krebs cycle) includes the presence of toxic levels of ammonia which leads to a wide range of symptoms mentioned by Dr. Chaitow: irritability, tiredness, headache, allergic food reactions especially to protein foods, and also at times diarrhea and nausea. Under continuous flight-or-fight reactions or shock reactions, the ATP cycle malfunctions. "Symptoms would usually relate to the effects of ammonia accumulation on carbohydrate metabolism, and upon the effect on neurotransmitters. Headache, motor problems, tremors, ataxia (shaky and unsteady movements), vomiting, liver enlargement, and even psychosis may occur," according to Chaitow.

PPS symptoms parallel symptoms of ATP dysfunction as well as other chronic debilitating conditions, especially Chronic Fatigue Syndrome and allergies.

The comparison of PPS survivors to marathon runners has been commonly made. The extra demands of a central nervous system functioning at 80 percent or less places the PPS person in the position of an athlete undergoing prolonged and strenuous activity. On several levels, the PPS survivor is in a constant state of fight or flight, partly caused by a faulty stress regulator and partly caused by overusing damaged nerves and muscles.

My *Bantam Medical Dictionary* says that ATP stores energy needed by cells and plays an important role in muscular contraction.

Amino Acids in Therapy notes that a deficiency in one mineral, **manganese**, can result in interference with this process. Perhaps, Jethro Kloss was right after all. Mineral deficiencies do cause nerve disorders and nearly everything else. Bananas, bran, celery, cereals, egg yolks, green leafy vegetables, legumes, nuts, pineapples, and whole grains, all food sources of manganese, might profitably be added to our diet.

In *The Miracle Nutrient Coenzyme Q 10, the Revolutionary Scientific Breakthrough That Can Strengthen The Heart, Boost the Immune System and Extend Life Naturally,* by Gerald L. Hunt and Emile G. Bliznakov, M.D., The President and Scientific Director of the Lupus Research Foundation, the mineral **selenium** and **vitamin E** were also mentioned as being important in the production of ATP. Ordinary tap water was said to be the most common source of selenium. Less common is brown rice. Common sources of vitamin E include dark green vegetables, eggs, organ meats, wheat germ, and vegetable oils.

Dr. Bliznakov's observations come from a slightly different angle on the ATP cycle. His focus has been on using coenzyme Q10 in the treatment of many diseases: lupus, muscular dystrophy, multiple sclerosis, cancer, heart disease, gum disease, Alzheimer's, AIDS, and aging problems of chronic fatigue, weakness, lack of energy. Coenzyme Q10 may well be a major player in restoring health to people with chronic illness.

In sports diets, Q10 has been added to increase muscle building, endurance, strength, and to alleviate fatigue. In self-help skin care circles, Q10 is one of the ingredients recommended to help rebuild and renew aging skin.

Coenzyme Q10, Dr. Bliznakov feels, is the critical factor in the production of ATP and the healthy functioning of all cells. "We know that CoQ is an integral part of the mitochondria, the subcellular components that are responsible for generating about 95 percent of the total energy needed by the human body. CoQ exists in the membranes of mitochondria, from where it performs its critical function, the manufacture of adenosine triphosphate (ATP), the basic energy molecule of the cell." He points out that Q10 is abundant in the organs requiring the largest supplies of energy: the heart, the liver, and the cells of the immune system. The human body produces Q10 on its own. However, it has been found in many studies that diseased states accompany low levels of Q10 production and Q10 declines with aging. Healthy states involve normal levels of Q10 production. In Japan and Europe, Q10 is only available as a prescription drug and has been prescribed as a part of therapy in a wide range of diseases. In fact, 10% of the entire Japanese population take Q10 daily, prescribed by their physicians. When Q10 has been added to other drug therapies, chemotherapy for cancer, drugs for heart disease, the other drug therapies work more efficiently to accomplish their purposes. Equally important, Q10 seems to protect against the unfortunate side effects of most drug therapies. In multiple by-pass surgery, it has been found to protect against further injury to the heart and to the brain caused by oxygen deficits during surgery.

Injury to healthy tissue is reduced when Q10 becomes a part of the treatment, and diseased tissue returns to health. Particularly dramatic and visible has been the reversal of gum disease when no other steps have been taken to treat the condition.

Quite dramatic have been the results of Q10 in mice studies. One hundred mice, 16 to 18 months of age, roughly equivalent to a human in his or her sixties and seventies, were divided into two groups. Both groups were kept on optimally nutritious diets. One group was selected as the control, the other, was injected with Q10 each week. "What soon became apparent was that the Q10 injected mice did not develop the normally expected signs of old age...their coats remained lustrous and healthy. They were bright eyed and active, and showed none of the immobility problems associated with old age in mice." Untreated mice lacked vigor, their fur grew sparse and patchy, and they began to die at an expected rate. By week 16 of the experiment, 30 percent of the untreated mice were dead while only 20 percent of the treated mice had died. By week 56, twice as long as they would normally be expected to live, 10 percent of the Q10 treated mice were still thriving. At week 36, all of the untreated mice were dead, but at that point 36 percent of the treated mice were still thriving. Q10 extends the life of mice by 50 percent in repeated experiments, and it's not only longevity that is prolonged, but youthful strength and health. The last mouse to succumb to death died at the human equivalent of 150 years of age.

In gerontology studies, it is commonly said that you are as young as your immune system. It has been observed that those people who live hale and hardy past the century mark were not subject to common childhood illnesses. I suspect that this is not the case with PPS survivors or others with chronic illness: like me, they have probably been subject to the full range of childhood illnesses sometimes including infantile paralysis. By the same token, it was reported that the immune systems of people subject to colds and the flu wear "scars" on their immune systems. PPS people, Dr. Bruno discovered, wear enough scars on their brains to look like a Swiss cheese. T-cells marshal the immune system response, marshaling up the war against foreign invaders and calling off the attack when the invader is dead. As people age, the T-cells become faulty. Richard Gerber, M.D., in *Vibrational Medicine* explained it this way: T-helper cells continue to function but T-suppresser cells fall victim to faulty regulation. The body, as with allergy, fails to distinguish between what is foreign and what is healthy. The immune system attacks healthy tissue frequently at the original site of damage. The same kind of thing happens in full blown AIDS. I have an annoying suspicion that this is a common pattern in chronic illness of all kinds.

Can Q10 reverse this process? Aged mice were injected with antigens to find out. One group was given a single injection of Q10; the other group was not. Both were injected with the same virus. The old mice who were not injected with Q10 responded with 130 units of antibody production. Old mice which had been injected with Q10 responded with nearly twice as much antibody production rivaling the 300 units of antibody produced in young mice with young thymuses.

66

Implicated in most aging studies is the importance of free radical damage. Free radicals have been implicated in everything from heart disease and cancer to aging spots, allergies and dandruff. Free radicals are produced by the natural processes of the body, ultra violet radiation from sunlight, environmental toxins, and the disease process. In the metabolism of fat, fat oxidation resulting in harmful fatty acids results. Harmful fatty acids contain unwanted and dangerous excesses of oxygen.

"CoQ (Q10) has the ability to manipulate oxygen. It can add or take away oxygen from a given biochemical combination, moving oxygen in or out of the mitochondria. It can increase oxygen levels when necessary, and reduce oxygen when necessary," according to Dr. Bliznakov. He also points out that other free radical scavengers that protect your system include **vitamins A, C, E**, pro-vitamin **beta-carotene**, and molecules containing **sulfur, selenium, copper, zinc**, and **manganese**. With the addition of these nutritional factors, the promise is a more youthful and healthily functioning immune system that will not attack the body's own healthy cells and will destroy antigens, foreign toxic invaders, or toxic by-products of cell metabolism like harmful fatty acids.

Considering that coenzyme Q10 was not identified until 1957, it could well be that the original German pharmaceutical studies in the thirties that attempted to identify the active ingredients in ginseng missed Q10 in the herb. Since Q10 works in much the same way as the adaptogen, ginseng, lowering or elevating whatever the body needs, and ginseng is known also to be a free radical scavenger of unknown properties, the properties might just include herbal forms of minerals and a very potent herbal Q10, Q9, or Q8 or some other form found in food sources. Coenzyme Q10 was first called ubiquinone, after the word ubiquitous, or omnipresent, since Q10 is ubiquitous in all life forms vegetable and animal. Perhaps, a particularly powerful herbal variety of Q10 exists in ginseng as it does less spectacularly in most raw foods, but quite plentifully in cooked beef heart. The vitality endowing claims of freshly juicing your own fruits and vegetables may just come from natural and strong concentrations of Q10 in addition to vitamins and minerals. Heat and storage reduce the enzyme content of frozen and canned juices. American nutritional deficiencies reported from the 1970s in *The Betrayal of Health* were linked with the loss of vitamin and mineral content in processed foods. Dr. Francis Pottenger, in *Pottenger's Cats*, found that "raw food factors," what Bliznakov would call enzymes, were responsible for keeping cats healthy and free from all chronic illness. Cats eating raw milk and raw meat from cattle also fed with raw food factors did not develop tooth decay, gum disease, diseased skin, arthritis, lung disease, or cancer. Cats fed raw foods died of two things: old age and cat fights. Both whole raw foods, freshly juiced raw foods, and enzyme supplements promise to right many wrongs about our health. Cooked and frozen foods may be major players in most chronic illness. Any cooking process destroys a part of the vitamin and mineral content of food. Cooking also destroys the enzymes necessary to digest food and the Q10 necessary for our own ATP cycle.

Early work with muscular dystrophy reported that one patient who had been told by his neurologist to expect to be in a wheelchair in two years was started on a program of Q10 and six years later was not only out of a wheelchair, but was swimming, playing golf, bowling, and conducting a vigorous legal practice. Similar hope exists for everyone with chronic illness.

Q10 has been one of the last things I've experimented with on myself. If I were doing it all over again, it would be the first. For one thing, Q10 is not known to have any toxic effects in nutritional supplement form. For another, I believe I did not respond to chiropractic, or acupuncture, or anything else very strongly because the basic energy carrier of my entire system was severely depleted. I was too weak to respond well to much of anything.

It seems that the warmer seasons bring with them lower levels of pain and less discomfort all around. But a sunny and warm summer has never had an impact on making much of a dent in my chronic fatigue or energy or strength. But I now believe that Q10 is slowly making a difference on a basic cellular level both in the summer and fall. I feel it: less fatigue, more energy, more ability to do things, and more desire to do more.

I first used the lowest possible dose, 10 mg, since maintenance doses were mentioned as averaging 10 to 30 mg.

Thirty milligrams were noted as maintaining and stabilizing gum disease; greater quantities averaging up to 100 mg were noted to reverse some severe conditions. It was also noted that one should never self-medicate and should seek professional guidance. The professional guidance I sought and trusted and still trust, suggested trial and error, small doses at first, gradually increasing, and noting the effects. The first four weeks it was 10, the second 20, and the third 30 mg. At 20 mg, my dentist had noticed no change, but no deterioration of the condition either. That was one thing I'd hoped for at low doses, but reversal of gum disease was not to be at those levels. Other gum disease studies supported the notion that maintenance begins at 30 mg; improvements begin at higher levels.

However, I did notice changes in muscular strength even with 10 mg. It was easier to walk up a few steps, for instance, after one week of taking 10 mg. For years, I struggled to walk up one step. Sometimes it was impossible unless I got down on my bottom and used my upper body strength to push off with my arms in the same way I got up from chairs. I used my arms. And my arms were not all that strong either. Now it is possible to stand from a seated position without using my arms for assistance. I can rise up out of a chair by using my right leg alone. Now it is possible to go up a flight of steps with my good right leg again. I use my arms to assist the ascent, but I make it. A whole flight of steps!

The obvious reason to me is that the ATP availability must be returning to prior healthier levels before the onset of chronic illness. My muscles must be contracting properly, and fasciculations have stopped in my upper body. They have not stopped in my lower body. I have more energy, and I have more strength. My general impression has been that Q10 helps make everything else I'm doing work and work better just as it seems to help in drug therapies. The effects of massage are much more beneficial after Q10 than before. Pain relief is immediate and lasting. Acupuncture is also a different experience after Q10 than it was before as is chiropractic. It might well be that my overall health was so low two years ago, that very little help came from a number of therapies and what did was very, very slow in coming. Q10 may be the fastest way to build up the body so that it may benefit from all areas of diet, nutritional supplements, and therapies of other kinds. Ironically, many herbal remedies discovered in Third World countries did not work in Third World countries, but they work in the United States. Why this irony? General health and nutrition are better in the United States, not perfect, just good enough to work. Just good enough might become excellent after Q10.

I'd love to see Q10 become part of AMA studies, homeopathic, naturopathic, and chiropractic studies in the United States for many chronic illnesses. Similar studies continue to be ongoing in Europe, Russia, and Japan. Over 80 pharmaceutical companies in Japan alone produce coenzyme Q10; few in the United States do, however. Bliznakov has analyzed the strength of U.S. products, and his recommendations are given in his work.

Any time I've worked more than two hours on a computer, not continuously, but a half hour per session, I've found my back and neck suffer the consequences. I work a half hour, and then I rest by taking an hour long soak in a hot bath with Epsom salts. I work another half hour, and I lie on my stomach, propped up by my elbows to stretch out my lower back and my shoulders. I lean into corners to stretch out my chest muscles and my shoulders. I practice the Johnny Carson turkey walk: chest out, double chin, shoulders back. I stretch out my neck. I do arm exercises, mild, and not very long. Even with this regimen, pain in the chest muscles, shoulders, neck accompany sitting at a computer. In the summers, I'd try a cell salt combination called *Nerve Tonic*, and I'd be pain free during those times. My voice also changed to something very different.

I was encouraged to try many things by my chiropractor, Dr. Guruka Khalsa who was versed in many areas of treatment both physical and metaphysical, and I was given the appropriate texts to read. She is versed in naturopathy and homeopathy and encouraged me to become an informed lay person in the areas of my interests. In addition to a sense of humor, I think knowledge must be the best weapon against chronic illness. Read about nutrition, read about health, read about therapies, read about resolving stress. A selected reading list is given at the end. I am grateful for what little I know, and grateful too that I was encouraged to be informed.

In colder seasons, for some reason, I'd forgotten about using the *Nerve Tonic* mineral salts. At first, I'd simply seen them on the shelf at my friendly health food store, asked my chiropractor about them, was encouraged to experiment, tried two doses, 6 little tasty pills, and noticed a couple of things. The rule of thumb I was given was—judge by the effects. Many individual responses take place. One thing will not serve for all. One effect I observed was that I had had a husky voice for nearly all of my adult life. People had difficulty hearing me. Speak up, they'd say. I'd speak up, and still people had difficulty hearing me. My voice had become throaty, husky, Clint-Eastwood-like. I had accepted it as a part of me and hadn't connected it with illness. My physiatrist had, though. He said that my vocal cords may have been implicated in nerve damage from either late effects or the original acute phase of the polio infection. Okay, it may have been something I had to gracefully or reluctantly accept.

After that was pointed out, I couldn't help but think of my step-father's voice. It was so husky that virtually no one could understand him. And too, he'd been subject to a physical nerve injury involving the whole right side of his body and his vocal cords. When I first tried *Nerve Tonic*, the first thing I noticed was a loud, audible, perfectly clear voice. I told my step-father about the *Nerve Tonic*, and he wanted to try a bottle. I sent him mine, and I forgot about the effects it had on me. Unfortunately for him, he either didn't try it, or it didn't work. His voice never changed.

One fall, I got another bottle. I wanted to see what would happen during a cold season, rainy damp and fairly miserable weather. So I took six tablets, on only one occasion.

On the evening of the day I took the tablets, I got very entertaining pains in my chest and shoulders and back. I hadn't experienced any pain for a week thanks to an expert massage by a masseuse. But on that night of taking the *Nerve Tonic*, the pains she had massaged out of me had returned. Then, the next day, I was pain free again. I also had warm feet for the first time ever during a cold season.

Here is one explanation: cell salts are homeopathic. Like some allergy shots, they can make things worse before they get better. The symptoms you try to alleviate get worse first, then improve. In fact, the worsening effect is a symptom that things are working. Dr. Schuessler's *Biochemic System of Medicine* found what he called twelve inorganic substances that affect different parts of the body. By trial and error on himself and his associates, he found treatments to be successful for a host of ailments.

Nerve Tonic (five mineral salts)

(1) *Calcium Phosphate* deficiency symptoms involves the experience of pain which is worse at night. Deficiency has been associated with cold hands and feet. Calcium Phosphate is the tissue salt remedy for "blood poverty and conditions associated

with imperfect circulation." "It assists digestion and assimilation and favours the building up of a sturdy, robust constitution...its restorative power will speed recovery and replenish the body's reserves of strength."

(2) *Iron Phosphate:* "It is the oxygen-carrier...takes up oxygen from the air inhaled by the lungs and carries it in the blood stream to all parts of the body thus furnishing the vital force that sustains life...Freely circulating, oxygen-rich blood is essential to health and life and for this reason Ferr. Phos. should always be considered, as a supplementary remedy, no matter what other treatments may be indicated by the symptoms." He points out that inflammatory pain calls for more oxygen. "It is an excellent remedy for ailments associated with advancing years...muscular strains, sprains."

(3) *Potassium Phosphate:* "It is the remedy for ailments of a truly nervous character... helping maintain a happy, contented disposition and sharpens the mental faculties." It is used as a remedy for nerve conditions of all kinds: "nervous headaches, nervous dyspepsia, sleeplessness, depression, languid weariness, lowered vitality, grumpiness and many other conditions which may be summed up in the modern colloquial phrase, "lack of pep." The mineral salt is said to be a "constituent of nervous tissue" and has a wide and powerful influence on "irritating skin ailments such as shingles, to correct the underlying nervous condition...helpful for breathing in nervous asthma...worsened by cold...and ameliorated by rest, warmth, and sometimes by eating."

(4) *Magnesium Phosphate* is known as the anti-spasmodic tissue salt. Deficiency symptoms are spasms and cramps. "This tissue-salt is of importance to muscular tissue ensuring rhythmic and coherent movement. Magnesium Phosphate is quick to relieve pain, especially cramping, shooting, darting or spasmodic pains." It relieves muscular twitching, cramps, nerve pains, stomach cramps, menstrual pains. These pains are said to be aggravated by cold and relieved by heat. Magnesium phosphate will "often act more rapidly when the tablets are taken with a sip of hot water."

(5) *Sodium phosphate* is an acid neutralizer. Deficiency is said to allow "uric acid to form salts which become deposited around the joints and tissues giving rise to stiffness and swelling, and other painful rheumatic symptoms." It is said to have an effect on indigestion, nervous irritability, and sleeplessness caused by indigestion.

Nerve Tonic is an alternative well worth considering. It's an inexpensive, possible solution that most people and physicians overlook. Even the alternative health professionals I consulted seemed unaware of its existence. Although I tried to discuss Q10 and amino acid therapies with many doctors also, no professional at the time was capable of helping. It had not occurred to me then that I had empowered myself by default to become better informed than they were. But if you're suffering, your motives in finding solutions are considerably stronger.

Of course, nothing I've written here is intended to replace normal physician advice or consultation, nor should it be construed as medical advice in itself. I am not a physician. Yet I am happy for what information I am able to gather, and I hope it will stimulate further study, further inquiry by both patients who have the liberty to inform themselves and by physicians to read outside of their fields, real physician supervised studies, real patient interest in looking into their own health. As the late Laura McCallum said very clearly, it is the duty of the PPS survivor to be as informed as possible about the PPS syndrome. I believe it is the duty of every person with chronic illness to do the same thing. It may be the patient who will help inform the doctor, not the other way around. In the PPS Newsletters presently in existence, it is more frequently the patient informing other patients. All of our observations and insights should be honored.

I hope that I live to see the day when all professional physicians and scientists share one office complex. The possibilities of understanding and the range of therapies that would emerge would be astounding. And if nothing more, the morning coffee or juice break would inspire very entertaining and mind-opening avenues of inquiry. As Robert Theobald has pointed out, the least informed people are in Washington, D.C., for one systemic reason. Power corrupts information, and absolute power corrupts information absolutely. The information is filtered through many aides, many industrial spokespersons, many special interests, and the information is diluted and corrupted by the process. A similar poverty of information exists when all people affected by treatment are isolated: the scientists, the therapists (plural), and the informed patients could form one heck of a task force to make new discoveries.

I think skepticism is warranted about all of the speculation I've made in this book as an individual. I am my own best skeptic. I can't quite believe many of the good things I've chanced upon. But chance observations lead to breakthroughs. A doctor at the Mayo Clinic, by chance, observed that women who had arthritis had their symptoms go away when they were pregnant. That led to the use of birth control pills in doses large enough to mimic pregnancy: a program to control pain came out of a chance observation. Maybe good things will happen from this. I hope so.

This winter may be a new experience for me. I'm looking forward to it. It's very pleasant having warmer feet, greater energy levels and strength even if I can't quite believe it.

Chapter 8

PLACEBOS AND AIS,
Acquired Immune Sufficiency

- What the alleged magnesium catch-22 is
- How the Catch-22 has been resolved in past Candida treatments
- Mineral wasters in your diet: hydrogenated fats, soft drinks, and caffeinated beverages
- Why you should be eating cold pressed oils and fish oils for your skin and Candida prevention
- Nystatin Rx: my thirty year hangover begins to clear in two doses and my energy soars
- Chelation or fusion in your doctor's office
- How damp weather, Candida and pain are related
- How diet and Candida are connected
- How placebos and skepticism are related
- Why you should expect to get well
- Why you should believe you are worthy to be well and neurolinguistic programming
- How bad luck may turn into good luck away from the cancer ward of the soul
- Why you should create a loving supportive environment for yourself
- My experience of never feeling worthy
- How we were rejected in the vulnerable years because of visible signs of paralysis or differences that didn't blend in with the crowd
- How Type-A personalities show symptoms of lack of self worth although it may appear the exact opposite
- How guilt, rejection, and sickness are connected
- What the Santa-Claus view of God is doing against you
- How reward-punishment fairy tales persist unconsciously
- Job and others who found themselves because of illness and disaster
- How the gift of being disappointed finally works for you
- How PPS and unresolved grief flood back with PPS
- Why we got sick in the first place
- Parents whose children die of leukemia and grief's demonstrable weakening effect on the immune system
- How AIDS and PPS are related
- How illness and lack of love, of self, from others, works
- How societal systems of education and medicine work to produce an environment of negative expectations

- How skepticism and self images are related
- How you can create a positive social environment
- Why we have AIDS of the soul
- Why the chemistry of love and acceptance should be studied and lived
- How to use your words to reprogram your immune system
- How to think WELL of yourself
- Why we should study people who stay healthy: my idea for a follow-up study
- How answers have come from studying health, not disease in smallpox, heart disease, cancer
- Why psychosomatic health, not psychosomatic disease, should be studied in Vilcabamba and everywhere else
- How you can stand on your own emotional feet even though you may not on your physical feet
- How having problems means you seek more answers

In Dr. Terrence Young's review of *Beating Chronic Illness*, he said that he found the data "impressively thorough." But he also felt that I had discounted various placebo effects on treatments that I had tried and neglected emphasis on the role of acetaldehyde in Candida colonization. Those things I intend to explore in this chapter.

Another issue that he emphasized was that **magnesium** and **potassium** deficiencies have been strongly implicated in recent studies of other neurological disorders including Parkinson's disease. Ironically, he pointed out that the body's ability to assimilate magnesium depends on the magnesium levels already in the body. That is to say, if you don't already have adequate magnesium in your body, assimilation may not take place. You have to have it in order to get it, a Catch-22, in his words, a double-binding life irony. To me, magnesium deficiency sounds like malnutrition syndromes in Third World countries: aid workers have found it hopeless to remedy. Once the damage was done, it seemed to be too late to rectify. I suspect a common link between malnutrition generally and Candida infection. It is almost a commonplace for doctors treating Candida to discover magnesium deficiencies in patients. But once the Candida infection is under control, magnesium levels return to normal. Perhaps in the rush to feed starving people, doctors put food in the children's mouths without thinking about the bloated stomach so terribly common among starving people. A bloated stomach is one sign of massive Candida colonization. If the infection were taken care of and the children were fed, maybe the damage could be reversed.

So the contention that magnesium deficiencies are irreversible is not unanimous among those who routinely treat Candida. William Crook, M.D., in *The Yeast Connection* noted that other doctors working to restore magnesium deficiency have succeeded by changing the diet of magnesium-deficient patients and treating Candida infection. Both are linked closely together. Crook noted that Candida raises havoc with magnesium absorption. Patients who take supplements pass the magnesium right on through their systems as if they are sieves when they are still infected with Candida. The Catch-22 may just be resolved when Candida is no longer confusing the process. Magnesium absorption begins to change as Candida populations decrease. Helpful dietary changes were found to improve magnesium levels in the bloodstream as well: soft drinks, caffeinated beverages, and hydrogenated fats in processed foods (they are almost omnipresent in processed foods) worsen magnesium metabolism. Avoidance of those foods and beverages make a difference in the body's ability to take in magnesium. Hydrogenated fats are almost omnipresent in canned foods and vegetable based margarines. Also improving the body's ability to accept magnesium were cold-processed vegetable oils, fish liver oils (both omega 3 and omega 6 oils), linseed oil, primrose oil, vitamin A, and the B complex. Interestingly, Candida patients in 2 out of 3 instances were reported to suffer from dry skin and a host of skin ailments. But when an "oil change" was attempted, the skin problems began to clear. Exploring the Candida connection may just be what the British Eczema Society needs to explore next. The British experience found that most frequently eczema cleared up when the bowel was "detoxified." I'd just bet on what got detoxed out of there, and its name begins with C.

This explanation for my own skin problems adds up to a simple chronological explanation for my experience. Multiple instances of broad spectrum antibiotics made Candida flourish. Candida wiped out my magnesium metabolism. Faulty magnesium metabolism set me up for dry skin, soft nails, and episodes of eczema that exactly followed visits to my dentist and dermatologist where I had been given more antibiotics. Magnesium deficiency led to nerve dysfunction. More population explosions of Candida ensued; post polio symptoms dramatically worsened. Then, I took one dose of nystatin, and I experienced mild improvements in post polio foggy thinking. The second dose and I felt as if a hangover I've been carrying around for years began to clear. I'd carried that fog in my head so long I thought it was normal to have it. It isn't, but you can't tell that until you experience the difference.

The third dose and energy levels soared. And such dramatic improvements are routinely reported by patients being treated for Candida as soon as treatment is begun, according to William Crook, M.D. in *The Yeast Connection.*

One caution: some doctors treating for Candida suggest small doses of fungicide to begin with. Large doses kill off so many of the critters so fast that the body can respond to the disintegrating Candida bodies allergically. With the allergic reaction is the possibility of people with other "unpleasant" symptoms becoming super "unpleasant."

I knew that, and I was wary. Even though I cut the dosage prescribed to half of what the doctor recommended but exactly what the pharmaceutical company suggested, my pain levels left the moon's orbit. At the same time my head began to clear, the pain levels became incredible. Unpleasant was nearly unbearable. The root cause was the quantity of yeast toxins flooding my system.

Dr. Young agreed with Dr. Maynard's feeling that toxins in one's environment might be profitably looked to. As Dr. Young said and as I knew from other sources, mercury deposits have been found in the brain tissues of both Parkinson's and Alzheimer's patients and are a prime candidate for nerve dysfunction. There is a very strong suggestion to my mind that toxins are part of the difficulty with neurological dysfunction and may play a role in chronic disease generally. The normal view is to remove the source of the poisoning. Don't expose yourself to mercurochrome, consider removing the silver-mercury amalgam fillings, take vitamin C, and hope you don't eat contaminated foods. **Mercury** is known to interfere with acetylcholine, and acetylcholine is partly responsible for mental alertness and good memory. Other possibilities involve chelation, which can be performed in a doctor's office, which helps remove heavy metals from the system. Chelation of zinc helps assimilation of zinc by the body; paradoxically, the chelation process can help bind the heavy metals already in the body, put them in solution and remove them from the body.

Even from the brain, I asked? Maybe. I then asked for and got a sublingual mineral diagnostic to find out if I still had basic mineral deficiencies in calcium, magnesium, and potassium. I also requested and got a hair analysis to determine deficiencies of trace minerals such as copper, selenium, and manganese. Sometimes heavy metal toxins also show up in hair analysis, and the results from hair analysis are believed to be most reliable by those who test for toxicities.

Oregonians who live under the dark monsoon and others living near bodies of water that produce humid climates are subject to another natural environmental toxin: **mold** and mold spores. In Oregon, mold spore count is high since molds thrive in dark damp places. All you have to do to get in trouble is rake moldy leaves, rake the grass, or breathe the air during moldy seasons. They love blasting into the dark and damp places of the human body. They thrive where "the sun don't shine." Raking grass stirs up millions of the buggers. The point made in *The Yeast Connection* was clear: close biological relatives of yeast aggravate Candida albicans.

Candida infected people frequently have to remove humidifiers in their homes, change jobs, change carpets, install lights and heaters in basements and closets, or disinfect sinks and bathrooms to reduce the molds. Individuals report sudden onsets of depression, nasal problems, skin problems, and a host of other difficulties when they are exposed to an explosion of mold spores. All I had to do to experience an explosion of pain one Christmas afternoon was to rake moldy leaves for five minutes. On the twelfth day of Christmas, many stupid ideas come to me.

Alcohol of any kind, all those tasty condiments, pickles, sauces, mayonnaises, the festive cheeses, soy sauce, baked goods, all contain products of yeast fermentation. Protection from Candida attacks is normally achieved in the first stages of Candida medication by simple avoidance of those foods and drinks. The hangover you would get from alcohol overindulgence is nothing compared to the hangover you carry around from the yeasters using your body to create their own parties. They turn your cells into stills for producing alcohol and aldehyde cocktails.

Protection from quantities of aldehydes that normally kill ninety percent of the rats exposed to high concentration was found in free radical scavengers, **vitamins C and B1**. The obvious thing is to remove yourself from the aldehydes that you have a choice in, or diminish them, and take vitamin and mineral supplements to protect yourself from the rest. The first important step to take in reducing aldehyde production in your body is to have the cause diagnosed, second to reduce the Candida cause, if that is in fact the cause, or at least to offer competition to the population of Candida. Other steps will be discussed later. Candida is very likely to be the chief criminal critter hiding in a dark and damp alley, its conspirators lurking in your moldy carpets, your basements, under your sinks, in the dark alleys of your body.

In both instances when I added free radical scavengers as supplements or therapies which helped toxin removal, and removed mercury amalgam fillings from my teeth, Dr. Young pointed out that **placebo effects** may well have played a role in my feeling better and getting better. "Placebo effects should not be discounted," he said, "and if they work, that's fine; the problem is solved."

Well, maybe. I am reluctant to consider the viability of placebo effects. For one thing, I'm an "old-born" skeptic, died-in-the-wool, full-time disbeliever unless it's proved to me, and the proof better be doggone good. When I had mercury amalgam fillings removed, I hoped for the best but expected nothing. I have grown accustomed to dead-end approaches. Although I want things to work, I've never expected them to. I've seen things work for a while and then stop working; I've also seen things not work at first, then work at a different time.

When I had the mercury amalgam fillings removed, my dentist said it was "all in my head." That was their original physical location. I remembered correctly that Durk Pearson had pointed out that placebo effects do not last beyond two weeks. In the study I had in mind, patients were given sugar pills and told they were morphine. Forty percent of the patients experienced pain relief for one week, but in the second week, only 10 percent were still experiencing pain relief. By the end of the second week, it was implied that no one experienced pain relief. A patient's expectations had limits when it came to that one study. Partly because of my own personality makeup, I wanted to believe that study. Forty percent of us are susceptible to suggestion; the rest are not. Of the 40%, only 10% persist for another week. Equally because of my skepticism, once one thing is proved, I doubt it.

Having just reviewed the morphine-sugar pill experiment, I again doubt it. Logically, other studies might just prove that there is a strong mind-body connection that could be or has been permanent: The mind might permanently effect its own cure in a very physical way. Of that, I have no doubt. What I do doubt is that it could happen to me. I've never believed anything all that easily; I have never EXPECTED to get well.

However, I do know others have. In *Quantum Healing* by D. Chopra, M.D., a cancer surgeon, wrote that he had opened up a woman who had had stomach cancer hoping to find a small cancer. Instead, he found cancer everywhere. It was inoperable. So he closed her back up, told her to go home and enjoy herself. He wanted only to make her final hours pleasant. Months later, the inoperable cancer patient returned. X-ray examination and blood tests showed her to be cancer free! This and many other examples mentioned by Chopra of hopeless cancer cases who were sent home from the cancer ward in the hospital turned up similar histories: people who stayed in the hospital expected to die and did. The people who returned home may have expected to die, but, once home, in a pleasant, loving, and positive environment, got better, sometimes with total remission of symptoms. I was envious of those stories. I wished I could have had an expectation strong enough to believe: to believe I was bound to get well sooner or later, or to have such a warm and loving environment strong enough to foster such a belief. The trick to me was learning to believe.

In other words, like the magnesium Catch-22, I had to have the thing I needed in order to take it in. In order to get better, I had to expect to get better. I had to believe I would get well before I could manage to believe it. I did not expect to get better, but I wanted to expect to get better. The thing that might just make for all health, the loving environment that, for example, Allen Taylor pointed out exists in isolated Russian communities where people normally live hale and hardy way past the century mark, was not in the majority position in my life.

As I was leaving Dr. Young's office where I had just had the most wonderful massage of my life, I was pleased to present my massage therapist, Allen, with a prescription from Dr. Young for two massages per month. My pleasure was partly that, if an M.D. makes an Rx for massage and classifies it as myotherapy, which it is, my insurance company might accept it for payment. The Scrooge in me and the low-budget life style I am forced to lead was pleased. I asked for ONE massage a month.

"The prescription says two," Allen pointed out.

"Right, well, I've never had more than one a month," I said. Actually, I'd only had five in my whole life. I couldn't afford them, and insurance normally did not cover them.

"I think you should have two a month," Allen said. "Two will really release all the stiffness, knots and tension you carry around. And let me tell you, you've got a lot of it."

"Do you really think I could have two a month?"

"You have the prescription."

"But what will I do without my old friend pain?"

"Get another friend," Allen said.

"I've never been that good to myself," I said. "Relieving pain has been a self-indulgence. Can I be that self-indulgent?"

I went away from that conversation thinking about it the rest of the day. I had jokingly revealed something new about myself to myself. I hadn't been all that generous to myself. In fact, I started wondering why I hadn't paid any attention to washing my paralyzed left leg. Wasn't it because, I rejected my left leg? I had rejected much about myself concerning polio and everything else. The next morning, I was up early with something dawning on me that had never occurred before.

I had never felt worthy. Period.

I had never felt worthy of many things. That's why I believed the placebo effect had never had much of an impact on any treatment I sought or did for myself. Yet that was changing and had been changing since August 1992. Furthermore, it had been changing little by little ever since I was in the same position that cancer patients were in who were sent home from the cancer ward.

The cancer ward I had been in was my former place of employment. Living with my department peers was an emotional cancer ward of the soul. It was a hospital of dysfunctional people who thrived on suspicion, envy, jealousy and distrust. I had "lived" in that atmosphere for twenty years. Anyone who had a special talent, an opportunity to teach a special class, a new idea, was envied, and treated with all kinds of negative feelings. When people wanted to talk about cutting the budget, I wanted to talk about increasing it and finding the revenue to do it with. As the tax base was eroding for public schools, I thought we could find other sources of income to do good things. This was met with derisive laughter. I was hooted out of the meeting. It was only one example of many.

And it was a common experience for at least three other members of a twenty-five member department. All three suffered with feelings of rejection. We were *personae non gratae*, people without merit or grace, in the words of one of the three. We were outcasts. Boy, did we feel that way. Although we had good home lives, and were loved by our spouses, we would come home dead on our feet, depressed that we'd been given the emotional shaft at the office. In different ways, I know we all internalized that sense of worthlessness. And the sense of worthlessness I had internalized at work was nothing compared to what had gone before.

In an untitled essay about PPS survivors' unresolved emotional issues by Carole Carsey, M.S.W. and Joyce Ann Tepley, M.S.W., masters in counseling and social work, it was pointed out loud and clear: "The person who left the hospital with less than complete recovery (from polio) had to cope with a fear that he was less worthy than others. One way to make up for those feelings was to prove otherwise." "Less complete recovery" is a euphemism for being called and treated as a cripple, Hopalong, a gimp, a basket case, and trash. I began to believe that this applied to anyone who was different physically or emotionally from someone else. It didn't happen just after leaving the hospital. Most of the people who went to the hospital had been overachievers to begin with. Thus, PPS survivors, nearly all of them, became super overachievers, to become as good or better than everyone else who didn't have a disability. The good news was that it may have made us more assertive and competitive, and therefore more adaptable to this society. But the bad news was not recognized by Carsey and Tepley.

I recognize it now. **Over achievement** was a smoke screen for covering up not being worthy enough. You don't overachieve when you feel worthy. You accept life a little more easily, take vacations physically and emotionally, neglect to honor deadlines, smell the roses rather than get to an appointment on time.

What I was stupidly telling myself was: I don't deserve to have two massages. I don't deserve to be without pain. I don't deserve to be well. I deserve to be punished. I don't deserve to be good to myself. In circulating the questionnaire printed at the end of this book, I asked this question: "Do you feel worthy enough to be well?" One respondent wrote, "I don't feel well enough to be worthy."

Anyone who has ever had extended chronic illness must have felt the same way. I must have brought it on myself. I must have done something wrong and my life must be wrong, for the universe to have given me polio in the first place. I thought polio was a punishment for violating a law that I didn't know existed. I was guilty that I was not innocent. I didn't know what I had done wrong, but polio felt like a punishment for a wrong doing. In the parental model of the universe that little kids have, when something bad happens to you, you must have been at fault. It's the Santa Claus view of God that persists at some unconscious level into adulthood. If you've been nice, you get presents. If you've been naughty, you get sick. We got polio; therefore, we must have done something to deserve it. Elizabeth Kübler Ross has pointed out that the reward-punishment view of God comes out in any person who has to confront death. Others have pointed out in *When Bad Things Happen to Good People* that the reward-punishment idea explodes. It's not big enough as an idea to understand the circumstance.

What I'm not so sure of is this: at what level does a small idea die when a bigger circumstance comes along to contradict it? The reward-punishment idea may die on some level of awareness, but I'm pretty darn

80

sure it does not go away deep inside. Everyone will notice that the real Goody Two Shoes, when she was very, very good, did not always get her other shoe. Childhood fairy tales of simplistic views of good and evil persist. There should be much more complicated fairy tales for adults. The story of the Biblical Job is one such tale that never made much sense to me, but is beginning to. When everything had been stripped from that man, he said, "Yet I will be true to mine own self." Something eluded me in that story. When I watched Tom Crawford, a college teacher and poet, be betrayed by his boss, I began to have a different view of the same circumstance.

Tom Crawford had been promised a job at a college by the boss of a department. When it came time for a committee acceptance of Tom, the boss did not bother to show up. Had the boss exercised his influence, his promise would have been fulfilled. Tom didn't get the job. For weeks, he suffered, suffered for not getting employment, suffered from a sense of betrayal that someone he valued and loved had not come through for him. Months later, he said, "There is justice; it gives you yourself."

I knew exactly what that meant, for him. In honoring a number of people who did not deserve to be honored, he was owned by that group of people. He did not own himself. He was someone else's man. In an important sense, he had sold his soul to the devil. But when that illusion exploded, he began to own up to himself and what he believed to be important.

Another author said it this way: "I have lost everything, but I have gained myself." A person cannot be true to himself or herself until s/he is no longer owned by the emotional lobbyists of the powerful majority. Disappointment and tragedy have a way of destroying the things that are not important and returning people, eventually, to what is important. "The things of this world" are negative, soul-destroying emotions and values. When they no longer have control of you, you can begin to love what is in yourself, rather than what others expect you to be. **Loving** yourself, loving others, loving the positive, believing that things are possible, are not popularly encouraged in politics, medicine, or education. They are not dominant attitudes. The dominant attitudes involve teaching others that they are unworthy, that sickness is expected and normal, and they will be lucky if they learn to march in step with whatever attitudes are currently in fashion before they decline and fall into hell and worse.

When people first get sick, they feel unworthy. People shy away from those in wheelchairs, who wear braces, who look or feel weak, who complain of not enough energy to do ordinary things. Everywhere you go, you are looked at. You are visible. You are treated as if you are a deadly virus invading the body politic. And you are attacked as foreign. If the illness is episodic and recurrent, eventually the unworthy feelings go deep inside where they lie dormant until post polio syndrome or some other recurrent bout with weakness comes around and knocks you off your feet again. In our senile immune systems, and our senescent attitudes about ourselves, we begin an **emotional autoimmune** attack on ourselves. It happens all over again, but this time you're old enough to figure it out, provided you look. An overwhelming sense of unworthiness floods back, and it's an occasion for real self discovery. I'm not okay, and the rest of the healthy world must be. We make jokes at our own expense. We become intentional clowns so at least we can control what the outside is laughing at.

You continue to participate in the very conditions that foster illness: poor self-images that are nearly totally unconscious show persistent signs of infection. We become allergic to ourselves and attack ourselves.

My speculation aired earlier in this work was that overachieving personalities preexisted the polio infection in the first place. I would say it differently now.

We got polio because we felt unworthy.

A sense of unworthiness made us sick.

We weakened our immune systems by expecting to be punished, by working ourselves to death, by choosing the hardest thing, by ignoring our diets. We Acquired a real Immune Deficiency Syndrome by thinking it on ourselves. Like a faulty immune system, we attacked ourselves with self-degrading humor. We put our systems in a chronic state of stress and overwork which weakened the natural ecosystem of the body's chemistry. Richard Gerber, M.D., points out that this is the common situation with parents who must watch their child die of leukemia. The depression which attends the grief has a demonstrable effect in depressing antibody production. It was not the parent's fault, and it was not our fault. But we felt that way. Unworthiness attitudes depress our health and make us sick.

It was not a conscious choice. But it was an unconscious one.

Much of the same unworthy self image is widely discussed among AIDS survivors. People get AIDS who are different, with different sexual orientation, abuse drugs because their society has not given them acceptance so they seek meaning in chemicals, or experience rejection because different personality or ethnic or racial characteristics are visible that don't blend in with the crowd. They don't feel loved or accepted. Dr. Gerber has pointed out that the immune system in childhood is preprogrammed to go wrong when children have not been accepted or have not accepted themselves. The life histories of those experiencing autoimmune disease amply demonstrate a life-long connection between a faulty self image and health problems. People with health problems have not been loved, and they have not learned to love themselves. They experience problems in the heart, chest, and thymus, the seat of physical nurturing, the site of the breasts; self defense and self protection; self love and self worth. My greatest pains have always been in my chest. That is where I carry the greatest amount of tension in my muscles. If I were a woman, I probably would have had breast cancer by now.

Those who are different sooner or later internalize rejection because they begin to believe what they hear others telling them: tall people, skinny people, smart people, dumb people. The only people who get automatic acceptance are average people, the Ronald Reagans who are the kings of being average. Those people win by a landslide. A Ross Perot would never make it into office. He is a little too "different," too intelligent, and has a sense of humor. Politicians never have senses of humor. They are the butt of jokes, the Dan Quayles, not the tellers of jokes. People learn to be wary and suspicious of "difference" in color, in race, in religion, in politics, in intelligence, in everything. They feel comfortable with stupid politicians.

As I thought through why I hadn't joyfully accepted the opportunity to get two massages a month, it all came rushing out. My Aunt Hanna was always uncomfortable around me, "The little genius, Step-Hann," she used to say, "oh, my goodness." And she shied away because I was smart. I thought about things that ordinary people took for granted, and I asked questions about them to no end. My father was never at ease around me. As a kid, I threatened his sense of authority. I saw ten alternatives to his one. My father was never pleased with, "But how about this alternative, and what about that?" He sat there sucking his teeth. And I interpreted those feelings as unworthiness. To my sister, I was her "crazy brother."

Our school systems don't encourage intelligence. They encourage conformity with the norm, the average. When I wrote papers that were just a little different, they were frequently received as threats: threats to the norm, threats to the authority of what teacher was in power, or threats to what bully ruled the peer group within the class. That didn't change in college either. You either conformed, or you didn't succeed.

One reason why I am getting better now is that I am beginning to think I am worth it, beginning. Worthiness precedes the placebo effect. And I think it is its most important precursor. I haven't felt that way for long, so it's a new experience to me. I began to trust myself in seeking to find answers. I began to trust myself in choosing to have my mercury amalgam fillings removed. I chose to help myself by reading, by nutrition, by massage, by chiropractic, by following the AMA's directions about less work and activity. All of those strategies add up to a growing sense of worthiness. I believe the people who are subject to placebo effects feel worthy to receive. Gerber generalizes this further. Health is the product of your own self image, your **unconditional acceptance** of yourself and others.

My life long skepticism about anything and everything has its origin in unworthiness. The certified genius that I am was too often received with reluctance; I was an egg-head, an outcast, an intellectual, a member of an "effete corps of impudent snobs," an alien in my own home. What I am coming to realize is that the loving environment my wife helps create, the loving care I've received from health professionals, the love I've begun to experience from my family, my son, my sister, my mother, and my few friends has begun to be my new environment. To my sister now, I'm "probably the most intelligent person in the world, one of the best writers, who knows nearly everything and can talk or write about anything." That's a heck of a lot different than the "crazy brother" of our youth. And it is, by chance circumstance of disability determination, my dominant environment. I am no longer living in a cancer ward. I am living in an environment of love.

I have always jokingly thought that the placebo was the best medicine in the world. But I rarely thought that I was good enough for it, or for that matter anything else.

I've been trying to prove myself my whole life. I have many things yet to prove. And I wish I could say with Carsey and Tepley, "we no longer have anything to prove." I'm working on it, maybe, just enough to help some things begin to work. But I'd take money on one thing: I'll bet that 98% of Post Polio Syndrome survivors, Parkinson's, Lupus, Chronic Fatigue Syndrome survivors, and others with life-threatening illnesses have a deeply buried sense of unworthiness that set up the condition, that followed the condition, and is, emotionally and physically speaking, an attitude responsible for our not getting better. There may be a literal link between AIDS and Polio presently being investigated in Irvine, California; I am certain there is an emotional link between an Acquired Immune Deficiency Syndrome of the soul and the post polio syndrome.

I believe too that there can be an Acquired Immune Sufficiency, AIS, (I coined the word), much more important, and much less mechanical than the placebo effect. I suspect there is a real **chemistry of love,** a real chemistry of joy and vitality, and that it would be registered in the system as health, proper antibody production, no immune dysfunction, and little adrenaline production affecting stiff muscles, weak muscles, and chronic pain. Can anyone with a chronic illness going to sleep at night say, "Thank God, I am who I am"?

In compiling answers from the questionnaire at the end of this book, there were two consistent inconsistences. Do you feel worthy enough to be well? was answered consistently with a yes, of course, what an odd question. The question, Would you consider yourself a Type-A personality? was also answered with a yes. The apparent contradiction was this: Type-A people who need to overachieve don't feel worthy enough or they wouldn't have to overdo things. You only tackle the impossible when you need to prove something to others or to yourself.

We are worthy to be well. We should say it as a statement, not a question. And we should repeat it until we begin to believe it. Julian Jaynes in *The Origin of Consciousness and the Breakdown of the Bicameral Mind* maintained that language is an unconscious function of neuronal commands. Our language on the most basic level is a system of signs given us by our midbrain to organize our physical and social survival. Our language is a metaphor of what our bodies are telling us; in chronic illness, our self images are a metaphor of a faulty immune system. Just as it works from the inside out, I believe it can work from the outside in. We can program the immune system by positive verbal commands to the body. We reeducate the neurons by what we say to ourselves.

What has been reported as the placebo effect is a mechanical way of talking about something much more profound. As a person thinks, so s/he is. This is a basic metaphysical or spiritual assumption. So I'd bet the forty percent of the people subject to placebo effects are the same people who think well of themselves. Get it, think well. And the vast majority not subject to placebo effects are people who think ill of themselves.

Among many disturbing trends in post polio research is the fact that post polio survivors who are subject to the syndrome of increasing weakness, chronic pain, chronic fatigue, chronic insomnia, and other things have been the only people studied. They have been the only post polio people studied. Only 20% of those who have had polio have been diagnosed with the syndrome.

Why didn't the other 80% get the darn thing?

Small pox vaccinations were not discovered by looking at the people who got the disease. The inoculation was discovered by looking at the people who did not get it. The American Cancer Society and the American Heart Association diets were not discovered by looking at the people with cancer and heart disease; they were discovered by looking at those who stayed healthy.

What are healthy survivors doing differently than those of us who stayed sick? I could make some easy deductions: they are not overachievers; they are not Type-A; they have good self images; they have good home lives; they pay attention to their diets; they have nothing to prove to themselves or anyone else; they have less visible signs of disability; they have been well received; they are average in intelligence (not too dumb and not too smart, or they pretend to be); and they have satisfying work lives where they have been professionally treated as a member of the club, not an alien germ invading and messing up things as they are. But I want to know, and I want to copy cat whatever that happens to be.

It is strange that educational psychology first and foremost still works with why people fail to learn, that teaching experiments have focused on why the class failed but not why the class succeeded. It is equally strange that parts of American medicine study disease rather than what keeps people well. Fascinatingly, the word psychosomatic means mind (psyche) in control of body (soma). Mind is in control of matter. In AMA dictionaries, the word is only defined as producing disease, nearly every diseased state. The fascinating part is that health may also be psychosomatic. Gee, why didn't that occur to the mind sets of the medical profession with the exception of Richard Gerber? The answer is simple: Health is not a part of their world view. It is not in the paradigm. It is not in the paradigm of enough educators or anyone else. It is invisible, and anything that promotes it is non-existent. Cells that are examined by pathologists are dead. Couldn't living tissue and health be looked at?

In ancient China, you paid the local doctor for keeping you well. If the doctor did not, the doctor paid you. Twenty percent of post polio syndrome survivors who became chronically ill would be very rich right now if that were still true. Eighty percent of polio survivors would have made the doctors millionaires by staying healthy.

A very wise old woman, Rev. Helen Brown, looked deeply into my eyes one day twenty years ago and said. "You chose to get polio yourself, and you chose it to give yourself a literal lesson that you could learn how to stand on your own two feet."

At the time she said it, I believed there was something to it in a literal sense. I wanted nothing more than to literally stand on both of my legs, and I believed that it would someday be possible. But that was not to be. Twenty years later, I have a new understanding of what she was trying to tell me. At the time, I couldn't have understood it. I sought acceptance in the eyes of others. Now, I am learning to stand on my own two emotional and intellectual feet. I have a few friends who catch me when I start to fall. I have also learned how to pick myself up from the floor. Since I was denied easy acceptance by my society, I have had no other recourse but to start giving it to myself. I stand alone now. I am beginning to honor and love everything, all the parts, that make up me.

And strangely enough, that includes what is called the post polio syndrome.

I have envied those with good health, and I have not always appreciated the special circumstance that polio gave me, not the first time, nor the second. But I am coming to understand and appreciate those states as a special gift. Without the problems, I would not have sought so many answers. I would not have even known what the question was.

Chapter 9

WHAT CAUSES CHRONIC ILLNESS;
What Should Be Studied

- Why you have been on a 30 year binge without knowing it
- How sunlight and the light of acceptance were denied people with chronic illness
- How darkness and early Candida infections are related
- How social difference and early rejections created an immune-weakening self image
- Antibiotics of the fifties: how the miracle drugs and vaccines affected meningitis survivors
- How poor self images can be worsened by visible signs of disability
- How we internalize social rejection
- How our immune systems are programmed by self images according to Richard Gerber, M.D.
- How above average grades and above average marks in illness are linked
- How we learned not to complain because nobody wanted to hear it
- How chronic bad tempers relate to the Candida induced alcoholic
- What joke-telling defense mechanisms are pro and con
- How slow processes of pseudoinfection & a sick immune system work
- How T-suppressor cells are depressed by alcohol's depressant effects
- What causes mineral deficiencies in attitude, diet, and Candida
- How chronic illness survivors were rejected by doctors and psychiatrists
- How being PPS fat further degrades self images and the Catch-22
- How disability is perceived by Social Security workers in my experience
- How being kicked out of the emotional cancer ward can work to your benefit
- Why suffering makes you look for answers and grow as a human being
- How the Dr. Jekyll-and-Mr.Hyde virus-bacteria-fungus-yeast quick change act works
- How you can anticipate treating a yeast to catch each of the many faces of a microbe
- What Royal Rife, AIDS, cancer, and polio may have in common

- My personal formula for discouraging the colonial and imperial interests of Candida expanding its influence
- Why we should honor a bug's right to live
- How the evolution of viruses and our own social conscience are related

Los Angeles Times in 1986 reported that Charles Swaart was arrested for drunk driving even though he had never drunk any alcohol. He was a teetotaler. Yet he was accused of going on binges when he suddenly would become hostile, irreverent, explosive. In fact, he and one Japanese man (reported in *Time Magazine* 1959) subject to the same thing were found to have massive colonies of Candida growing in their intestines, producing their own alcohol within their own bodies, and numerous quantities of pickling aldehydes. In both instances, their doctors said they had been on a twenty year binge without having drunk one drop of booze. (William Crook, M.D., *The Yeast Connection.*)

I believe that is exactly what happened to people subject to the post polio syndrome and chronic illness. Every infant by six months of age shows evidence of Candida presence. For breast-fed infants, the natural friendly bacteria in breast milk protects them. For children reared in sunlight and in the light of easy acceptance and love, they grow healthy and strong. They are subject to few illnesses. They are touched and loved. They are given good diets rich in minerals and vitamins and other nutrients.

But I believe the chronic illness pattern is different. We were not breast fed, lacked being given the natural protection conferred by L. acidophilus and other friendly bacteria in a mother's milk. Instead, we were one way or another not subject to much of anything that was friendly in our diets, our natural environment, or our social environment. We were untouchables. We began to overstress our bodies looking to prove our worth in the eyes of the world. Dietary deficiencies developed and our immune systems were weakened. In this state, we were subject to greater than average infectious diseases of childhood. Each one of them weakened the immune system further and left scars.

We were then given new broad spectrum antibiotics developed in the forties, the mycin group of drugs. Each dose of antibiotics weakened us further. We were given vaccines with neurotoxins in them. At some point afterwards, we became sick. If we got polio, we brought to polio a poor self image, and, if we had a visible sign of crippling, we limped, could not hide a paralyzed hand or arm, used wheelchairs or crutches, and were subject to rejection and a worsened self image. If we had no physical sign of disability, something made us not blend with the crowd. We didn't fit in because we were different in some way, ethnically, racially, in religion, in personality, in mental ability, in appearance. We were treated as foreign germs invading the healthy body politic. We fought back by overachieving all the more. We would prove we were worthy.

But secretly we had already internalized the rejections of others into self doubt. We became our own worst enemy. We attacked ourselves in the same way we had been attacked. We developed a sense of humor that jokingly made fun of ourselves. On an emotional level, we recapitulated what was done to us from the outside. Ontogeny recapitulated the phylogeny of our social experience. The inside became a mirror of the outside. We attacked ourselves in the same way a paralyzed immune system can no longer distinguish between what is good or bad, foreign or healthy. Our immune systems were programmed by our attitudes to destroy the person and the body or mind that didn't fit in.

Every mental thing was connected with every physical thing. As above, so below, as within, so without, as Hermes Trismegistus said. We interpreted the outside and applied it to the inside. We continued to be subject to further illness. As we earned above average grades, we earned above average marks in illness. Each illness was accompanied by broad spectrum antibiotics. Anyone getting sick who was also given large doses of antibiotics grew a massive colony of Candida albicans from the very beginning. Candida put us on a twenty to thirty year binge without taking one drop of alcohol. But we cleared the cobwebs from our minds and learned to keep a stiff upper lip. We learned not to complain about feeling lousy because everyone we told felt it was a sign of weakness. So we learned how to look strong by acting assertive and brave. We repressed our feelings, our sadness, our weakness, our anger and projected them onto the outside. We developed chronic bad tempers in the same way alcoholics did. For us, it was a defense mechanism and a way of survival. The bad temper warded off enemies who wished to attack us; it also pushed away potential friends who might have supported us.

Autopsies of our deceased brothers and sisters who had acute polio infection showed persistent signs of infection dating from 5 to 40 years after the onset of polio. Brain lesions were discovered in the hypothalamus. At first, they were small little areas of damage. But they grew with the accumulation of acetaldehydes, allergic reactions to damaged tissue, and autoimmune attacks. For years, we experienced no symptoms as the area of damage grew, or we denied our symptoms because they were unwelcome in society, our family, ourselves. "You must be tired, dear," my mother used to say. The damage grew from several causes: the pickling and cross-linking effects of aldehydes produced by our own Candida factories; persistent infection by the chickenpox virus that had taken residence in our spines; persistent infection in some cases maybe by a "polio" virus itself; an unresponsive or paralyzed immune system which mirrored the paralysis on the outside of our bodies and our paralyzed emotions. We were unable to ward off foreign germs; instead, our immune systems learned to tolerate the presence of the viruses because at different times our immune system was pickled by the Candida stills working overtime to recklessly party and damage things inside our systems, our hypothalamus, our central nervous system, and our muscles.

The T-suppresser cells were depressed by the depressant effect of alcohol on a cellular level. Our unresolved grief over illness depressed them further.

We developed mineral and vitamin deficiencies as a result of not caring enough about ourselves to take care of ourselves or eat well. Instead, we responded to the Candida as if it were Dionysus: we fed it what it commanded us to—sugar, honey, vinegar, pickles, yeast breads, baked goods, fatty acids, and we drank sugared soft drinks until they went out of style. We behaved as if we were the Dionysus of legend: we had wide mood swings, some joyful, some terrible. We like Dionysus were torn apart by internal revels.

We developed further signs of deficiency by the presence of Candida disrupting what nutrition we tried to take in. We took birth control pills and other steroids which worsened the condition.

We went to doctors who at first could not find out anything wrong and blamed our problems, partly correctly, on psychosomatic complaints. And the psychosomatic complaints were themselves a part of the problem. Our minds had helped create an emotional and physical ecosystem that was doing us no good. Then, we were referred to counselors who weakened our self image further by thinking we were crazy.

Then, we were diagnosed as having chronic illness: chronic weakness, dry hands, cold limbs, depression, insomnia, breathing difficulties, speaking difficulties, and problems with thinking and remembering. Our muscles were turning to fat as a result, and we couldn't lose weight because our weight regulator was damaged. Our self images worsened because we were fat. We tried harder.

Our employers who had always considered us superwomen and supermen who were stupidly willing to do extra work without pay would not believe us. Social Security people who interviewed us made us fill out forms for the mentally deranged "just in case you aren't approved for a physical disability." This irritated an already entrenched negative self image.

We were unable to work at previous levels and were considered malingerers. We didn't look sick, so no one believed we were. Then, we were given a name for some disease with no known cause: Post Polio Syndrome, Chronic Fatigue Syndrome, Yuppie Flu, CFIDS, Lupus, Multiple Sclerosis, Depression, Aging. Giving an illness a name offered a sense of assurance that something was indeed wrong, but the name itself relegated illness to an incurable category. Then, we may have showed up at work with a cane, or in a wheelchair, and our former "friends" didn't know how to handle it. Some of us had after-images of getting polio the first time, wearing unsightly braces, embarrassed to go to swimming pools, and made fun of as gimps, cripples, and lepers.

We had never had many friends, and now we had fewer. We tried to process unresolved stress in our past from our never accepting losses as permanent. We had to face loss once again, and that was painful. We had learned not to think of ourselves as worthy. That was why we did extra things and walked an extra mile.

We tried many things and were told we would gradually lose what little we had left. We were told to expect to stabilize at best.

Then, some of us were advised to quit working because it was, in fact, impossible to work at former levels and sometimes impossible to get out of bed; we were sentenced to home-imprisonment with a loving spouse. We were kicked out of the cancer ward of the soul, a work environment that had never given us approval easily. It was an environment that sanctified the strong, but we were no longer able to make that team.

But now we were at home where we could create our own world. Brer Rabbit was thrown into the briar patch, where he started to improve. Even with intense pain, he no longer had to hear the catcalls he heard at work about Hopalong and stumpy. He started to feel better although the body wasn't cooperative at first.

Then, since he felt better about himself, he started paying more attention to his diet. He started reading and trying things. The isolation that sickness imposes on the individual begins to make one responsible for oneself. The isolated person stops listening to the impossible. He decided to know enough to find something to help. Lots of temporary things started to help on a short term basis: vitamins, minerals, better food, chiropractic, massage, acupuncture, amino acids, Q10. They helped manage the pain and the damage done by stiffened muscles, unequal leg lengths or hips that wouldn't allow you to sit straight.

This sick person decided to have other unrelated health concerns improved because he felt good enough about himself to be good to himself. He decided to boost his own immune system with herbs and enzymes and love, and this Brer Rabbit grew stronger in muscle strength, endurance, and energy. He was diagnosed with Candida, and a 30-year-old hangover broke up like the clouds scattering after a storm. And gradually, gradually, the self image grows brighter and stronger and more beautiful until the sick person can finally say, I am worth it. And the episodes of health lengthen and lengthen and lengthen until life is fully worth living for the first time in fifty-one years. As an old man, he gives himself what he had wanted from his childhood family. He begins to practice what healthy people have always done.

William Crook described the yeast form of Candida albicans as an ovoid microbe at the beginning of his book, and there are pictures to illustrate that form. Also present are picture illustrations of mold forms. Yeasts were presented as roughly circular in nature. Molds were then presented as circular with branching tubes which are known to invade cells and become the cause of allergic triggers in some individuals they infest.

Near the end of his book, there is another set of pictures that Dr. Crook did not seem to connect to his first discussion. In a section inspired by mycologists, four more illustrations appear under the heading "Candida Albicans—a Dr. Jekyll and Mr. Hyde." In this section, the Candida was demonstrated to have at least four basic forms. First, a blastospore (rounded), second a budding blastospore transforming into (sometimes) two rounded forms. This was identified as the yeast replication cycle, the normal cycle. They look very much like the rounded yeast you see for baking bread. But a second form of Candida can also emerge: this form does not progress into two equal forms, but it grows a microscopic tube called a beginning hypha. A beginning hypha resembles the mushroom fungus; it has the same shape. It bears a striking resemblance to illustrations of molds which were earlier said to be a different but related life form. A fully formed hypha grows an elongated tube, at which time it resembles a mushroom with a very long stem or a rodlike form. Sometimes the hypha grows very long branches (the illustration shows seven) and it resembles a tree or an orchid plant.

Dr. Crook pointed out that he had used his thinking about such forms to treat Candida; single-cell yeast Candida is believed to respond to Capricin in mild infections, or the therapeutic use of garlic in any form, nystatin, or Nizoral.

Dr. Crook observed that some patients don't respond to Capricin, garlic, or nystatin, and he added another medication like Nizoral, which unlike nystatin is carried into the bloodstream. Sometimes both medications are used in the beginning in patients with extreme symptoms because it has been demonstrated that Candida can switch forms from yeast to fungus very rapidly like a quick-change Dr. Jekyll and Mr. Hyde trick to evade being killed.

It seems to me that garlic should always accompany the treatment as well as zinc and the amino acid, L-lysine. In a book called the *Cancer Cure that Worked*, Royal Rife, the inventor of the Universal Microscope, was able to demonstrate that all viruses he studied took pleomorphic forms. That is to say, that all viruses can escape detection and evade treatment by changing into bacterial forms, many bacterial forms, and many other forms. Bacterial forms can evade broad spectrum antibiotics by transforming back into viral forms or fungoid forms. In fact, Dr. Rife maintained that all microbial life forms are subject to pleomorphism, many formed, as an evolutionary survival mechanism.

Disturbing to me is that the cancer virus, which he called BX, has at least two different manifestations: HIV and BX. One is associated with AIDS, the other with cancer. One line of ongoing PPS research in Irvine California, Mrs. Faith Wyckoff informed me, has hypothesized that the AIDS virus causes the post polio syndrome. That does not make me happy.

What does make me happy is that Royal Rife said that the fungoid phase of the cancer virus resembles the mushroom at one stage and the orchid at another when it begins to send out branches. I have an awful suspicion that one of the 79 strains of Candida fungoid yeast is a member of the Dr. Jekyll and Mr. Hyde cancer-AIDS group.

The reason for my happiness is this: I have been diagnosed twice as having the Candida infection. Each time I've taken one of the caprylic acid drops, my symptoms receded. After trying nystatin, some of the symptoms receded dramatically as others worsened. At the same time, I added **lysine** supplementation to confuse the metabolism of the viral phase and **zinc** to prevent its viral replication process. I also put more garlic in my diet and took aged raw garlic for the antibacterial properties. Garlic has been demonstrated to be more effective than prescription antibiotics in wiping out unfriendly bacteria but without the unfortunate effects of wiping out friendly acidophilus and other friendly gut bacteria. In fact, Carper in *The Food Pharmacy* quotes one researcher as saying: "Garlic has the broadest spectrum of any antimicrobial substance we know of. It's antibacterial, antifungal, antiparasitic, antiprotozoan, and antiviral." Well, you could guess how I announce my presence from five feet away and more.

I have also added **acidophilus** capsules to my diet to give Candida and other unfriendly buggers great competition. Most unfriendly microbes can't take an acidic environment, and acidophilus provides one through producing small quantities of benzoic acid. It also produces acidophilin, a broadspectrum anti-microbial substance. And it provides an oxygen environment through its production of hydrogen peroxide. Candida and other unfriendly bugs can't exist either in an environment of **oxygen** or **light.**

My personal formula for establishing peaceful coexistence with the unknown antigen has this rationale: part of the many-formed Candida Quick Change Artist troupe will be killed off or digested in its yeast-fungus phases, part in its bacterial phases, and part in its viral phases with a constellation of fungicides, natural antibacterial foods, and mineral-amino acid supplements. I don't think the innocent, white-colored traveler Candida, who resembles Candide, will be getting Pangloss in quite as much trouble. And Candide's significant other will not lose so much of her gluteus maximus the next time. I'm very close to beating polio the second time around.

I don't think Candida can be destroyed nor that it should be. I believe it as well as all other microbes have a right to be here. But I do think the microbe population can be pruned down to a reasonable size that is not harmful. I think there is a reason for its being in the human body, and an all-out nuclear war may not be the best choice. It seems that the Ebola Zaire virus has mutated into a reasonably amicable Ebola Reston. And it has good reason to do so. If a virus remains deadly to its host, it will die off with the host. But if it establishes a more civilized relationship, tolerating the right of the host to live, it too will live. I feel the same way about Candida. Candida may not only be the major player in chronic illness, Chronic Fatigue Syndrome, Post Polio Syndrome, Lupus, and other conditions. It may also be the chief source of our muse, lifting us to new heights; and sometimes, when it decides to expand its empire to the extent of outnumbering every cell in the human body, giving us a long-term binge head-ache, aches and pains, and inability to think. Like balanced levels of his-tamine, enough histamine and you can put things in their proper logical place; but when you have a histamine excess, you become overwhelmed physically and mentally. As constitutions recognize the rights of races, of women, of children; as countries recognize and learn to tolerate the others, I think I can learn to tolerate and get along with a tiny creature. I believe one of the purposes being served by illness is to learn how to get along, to get along with our human environment, our emotions, and our microbes.

One thing that should have been done a long time ago was a compara-tive study of post polio syndrome survivors with people who got polio and stayed healthy. The same thing is true with people subject to chronic ill-ness generally and people who stay healthy. We should have known what their life and medical histories were. But we didn't, and we don't know. Comparative population studies can reveal many useful things. It was how Nathan Pritikin, the work of one person, turned the American Heart Association's thinking around about the uses of diet and exercise to control heart disease. Pritikin may not have been given credit for it, but if he hadn't spoken at one AMA conference, the world would be a different place. We all know what to do now, and what we know came out of looking at populations not subject to heart disease.

At the end of this book you'll find a list of questions that suggests comparing the lives and medical histories of people with chronic illness to people who stay healthy. Although The Easter Seals Society in California, some individuals in Oregon and the South, did circulate the questionnaire, very few people took the time to fill it out. I also posted it on electronic bulletin boards, but bulletin board managers don't care for questionnaires. Of the twenty or so responses I did collect, I did find the suggestion of the pattern I believe to be true in this book. I offer the questionnaire at the end in the hope that someone will take up the idea as is or with modification. Shouldn't we find out what people do to stay healthy? Shouldn't we know as much as possible about the people in Vilcabamba, Ecuador, who never become ill with anything? Cultures and groups that promote acceptance of others may not have overworking Type-A personalities at all.

Bonnie Presley wrote to me about her husband who did have an acute infection of polio: "We can't figure out why—(her husband is not subject to PPS). He is overweight, does not eat a great diet, and does very little exercise. Yet he is one of the happiest, most self-reliant people I know. His attitude towards life is a daily lesson for me, and I feel that he would have been this way even if he had not had polio. He is sort of a Type-B, but not passive, does that make sense?"

Yep, it does to me.

Chapter 10

MOLYBDENUM:
Pain, Strength, Energy, Foggy Thinking

- How molybdenum can affect areas of pain and turn them into heat
- How molybdenum can restore muscle strength
- How molybdenum chelates out heavy metal toxins and acetaldehydes
- How molybdenum clears sinuses and restores mental clarity
- How trace mineral deficiency was said to be the cause of Multiple Sclerosis by Edgar Cayce and the role of digestive upset
- How Candida is responsible for mineral deficiencies of all kinds and how laboratory analyses of my hair and saliva confirmed suspicions of deficiency syndromes; what deficiencies I had and what others with chronic illness are likely to have
- Why the FDA should have balanced Advisory Committees reviewing nutrients and everything else
- Why informed consumers should be on Advisory Committees with voting power
- Why small growth and health food and supplement industries should be on FDA Committees
- How health care costs can easily be reduced
- Why it is to our benefit to have many choices as patients and consumers
- How informal alliances in FDA, AMA, and large industry artificially raise prices and what would happen with real competition

When I started prescription nystatin therapy to take care of the Candida infection in my mouth and gut, I had high expectations that something good would come of it. I had no idea just how dramatic an antifungal treatment could be. The first day made a dent in clearing a 30-year-old hangover, and that clear headedness continues. Equally dramatic was a worsening of growling, gas, and bloating which followed every dose. Only in the second week of taking nystatin did I experience less gas or growling when I ate Candida-nourishing foods: that is, Candida nourishing foods tend to be junk foods, hydrogenated fats, sugar, refined carbohydrates, vinegar, wine, beer. Eating mushroom soup, for instance, which contains nearly all the foods that Candida thrives on (yeast products, sugar, mushrooms, and hydrogenated fats) made Candida during the first week of therapy go wild, wild enough for me to be convinced that I had made the richest discovery of natural gas in the world.

As William Crook and Orian Truss had observed in *The Yeast Connection* and *The Missing Diagnosis*, only small doses of fungicides should be used therapeutically when patients have been diagnosed as having other "very unpleasant" symptoms. The reason stated was that, clinically or unclinically speaking, "unpleasant" can become superlatively unbearable. The cause suspected was increased accumulation of yeast by-products in some unidentified way irritating the systems of people so infected.

That was precisely my experience. At the same time my head cleared, pain levels soared during the first week of taking nystatin, and I empowered myself to cut the dosage in half, half of what my doctor prescribed, but what the pharmaceutical company had recommended. But even with this timid dosage, my pain still skyrocketed slightly beyond the Voyager space vehicle in my chest and back, and in my newly weakened right leg. Also, muscle twitching intensified beyond anything I had ever experienced before. My weakened right leg was turned into a snarling writhing mass of very active fasciculations. In fact, my experience was a reenactment of my observations in taking homeopathic allergy shots. Both therapies made my post polio symptoms dramatically worsen, especially pain. In a sense, I believe that some homeopathic remedies that operate by giving you a hair of the dog that bit you may not work well for those with painful symptoms. The hair tends to turn, in my experience, into a monstrous hairy problem.

In presenting my feelings to a Post Polio Support Group in Salem, one wise PPS survivor echoed one of my statements about nystatin. I had said, "Nystatin is said to 'kill everything it touches.'" Hudson, the wise PPS survivor, said, "Kill everything it touches?" That started me thinking. Presumably, nystatin kills every Candida albicans yeast cell it touches. However, it is a commonplace observation in natural modes of healing circles to note that the hazards of taking prescription antibiotics is this: they kill pathogens literally, but they also can harm healthy tissue. I thought about this for days. Out of it came this observation: garlic is not said to kill anything. It is said to reduce the population of pathogens, reduce, not kill. The pathogens in **oregano** and **garlic** studies and other studies are observed to be reduced in population, reduced by count, said to melt, or wilt, but not for the species to die. The same has been observed with **acidophilus** studies.

It occurred to me that I could pursue a natural approach to dealing with Candida. What if Candida, like bacteria, grow resistant to something that attempts to wipe out the species? For one thing, the species will mutate and will no longer respond to the drug. For another, nearly every post polio survivor I had talked with and corresponded with has said this one amazing thing. Prescription drugs produce allergic reactions in them. This led to a chain of deductions.

Antibiotics and other hormone influencing drugs like steroids are well known in Europe, Japan, China, and Russia to weaken the immune system. A weakened immune system is commonly associated with autoimmune disorders. Post Polio is presently being investigated as an autoimmune

96

disorder acting like arthritis of the muscles and nerves. In autoimmune disorders, the immune system begins to confuse pathogens with healthy tissue, which may account for the brain lesions Dr. Bruno discovered by reexamining the autopsies of post polio victims who died in the 1950s. Similar slow infectious processes, or pseudoinfection processes, may be triggered by a host of synthetic drugs.

After synthetic drugs, Candida is known to flourish. Candida is responsible for flooding the system with an accumulation of toxic acetaldehydes. Acetaldehydes are known to poison tissues.

A weakened immune system may not be able to distinguish between an accumulation of acetaldehydes in the brain, the spinal cord, the joints, and the muscles and tissues which are weakened, but otherwise healthy. So the immune system, partly drunken by Candida-produced alcohol and its pickling by-product, acetaldehyde, begins to clean up the mess. The immune system believes it is doing its job properly, but it is a drunk driver, crashing into old cells in the myelin sheath, the muscles, the brain itself, the nerves to the muscles, and literally slowly eating them alive. It occurred to me to be more appropriate to use smelling salts to sober them up. I believe that mineral and food substances work in exactly that way: Garlic, **oil of oregano**, and **minerals** that directly affect the aroma centers of the hypothalamus may do just that.

I then talked this over with Dr. Carol Cooper, D.C., because I wanted to try a natural approach. She said that she would get back to me if she ran into anything that might suit my theories. I wanted to peacefully coexist with my bugs, not destroy them.

Fatefully, I got a call back the next day. A salesperson from Nutri-West had just dropped by one day after our talk and left a mineral, molybdenum, for me to try. It wasn't a medication; it was a nutrient. Dr. Cooper then called me to ask if I'd like to give it a try. I hadn't liked the experience of worsening symptoms under nystatin, so I was open to a new approach.

I decided to try **molybdenum** at Dr. Carol Cooper's suggestion simply because it had a blanket reputation for breaking down yeast by-products into forms that the body could excrete. That was all I knew about it and really had no expectations of what it was going to do, or why.

I started molybdenum therapy as per Dr. Cooper's advice: 100 mcg three times a day dissolved on the tongue or chewed in the mouth.

The first tablet was fascinating in its effects. My energy surged, a common clinical observation made by Dr. Walter Schmitt in "Molybdenum For Candida Albicans Patients and Other Problems," I later discovered. Three days after taking molybdenum, Dr. Cooper had sent me the clinical study in the mail since she knew I was interested and knew I believed Candida was chiefly responsible for my chronic symptoms of pain, weakness, and fatigue.

97

Dr. Schmitt mentioned that clinical studies normally showed that patients with chronic fatigue soon became better, that muscular weakness turned into strength, and that pain levels declined. His observations are so good that you must read them in their entirety. His chemical explanations are both brilliant and clear, and they make good common sense for chronic illness generally. With his permission, I've reprinted them at the end of this book.

My experience provided a fascinating confirmation to my suspicion that Candida was chiefly responsible for what was called the post polio syndrome. On the second day of molybdenum, I experienced copious sweating on my back, one seat of my chronic pain. Over the entire area of back pain, perspiration poured out of me, and I experienced heat in my neck muscles. Then, the next day my back pain was totally absent! In scoliosis studies, it has been believed that curvature of the spine triggers night sweating, but I am beginning to believe that other explanations are possible for day and night sweating. Sweating may be a part of the body's own detoxification processes.

It was difficult to believe but wonderful to experience pain turning into pleasant heat. Within seconds, changes can be noticed. Within hours, remission can begin.

That evening, I experienced a sensation of warmth in my chest. This was odd. My pectoral muscles in my chest were, that's past tense, the site of my most intense pains. But I was not experiencing pain in my chest, I was experiencing pleasant warmth just as if I had grown an internal heating pad. What was happening?

The next morning I awakened to much lower levels of pain in my chest. The storm had passed, and something was responsible for it. I also noticed the chronic pains in my right leg were gone. Nystatin had intensified those pains somehow, but molybdenum had taken them away.

I had the article by Walter Schmitt on the table, and I began to read it carefully looking for the answers. And I found exactly what I needed to find: Molybdenum is chemically responsible for breaking down acetaldehyde into acetic acid. Acetaldehyde cannot be excreted from the body; it accumulates. Acetic acid can be though, and the body naturally removes it or it changes into acetyl coenzyme A, a major player in the body's energy system. With a simple mineral, it was possible to transform a poison into a source of energy and strength. A chemical evil transforms itself into a source of living energy.

As Dr. Schmitt explained it, acetaldehyde accumulations in tissue are responsible for weakness in muscles, irritation, and PAIN. When they begin to break up, the pain breaks up. I was so excited I called Dr. Cooper to thank her for telling me about molybdenum, but I wanted to know why I had experienced the sensation of heat. How in the world could something so totally unpleasant turn into something so wonderfully pleasant?

Her explanation was quite simple: "Chemical reactions produce heat." So you mean as the acetaldehyde accumulations break down, I would feel the heat?"

Yep.

Then, the following day I got the lab reports I wanted for my own mineral analysis. I wanted an analysis to confirm one hypothesis I had about mineral deficiencies causing or accompanying nerve dysfunction. I found exactly what I expected to find and several things I did not anticipate at all.

Magnesium and **potassium** levels were depressed. So was iron. That I expected. I had known that Candida interfered with mineral metabolism, chiefly magnesium, but also with others. Candida was responsible for that. All other minerals, including toxic metals, were within safe ranges, or normal to desirable ranges with the exception of phosphorus which was slightly elevated. I had expected to find aluminum in toxic levels because of Dr. Maynard's thinking on the matter that environmental toxins may play a role in PPS as they do in many other neurological disorders. But that contention was not supported in my case. I also expected to find toxic levels of mercury, but that wasn't the case either. However, copper and phosphorus were elevated off the scale. Okay, I said to myself, I'll cut down on the red meat, the red wine, the yellow cheeses, the dairy products, and the yeasts. The what? The yeasts: once again, to my way of thinking, Candida turned up to be guilty. Candida is a yeast, and yeast by-products are lousy with phosphorus; excessive copper is associated in some unexplained way with Candida infection as well.

However, I did not eat much of any yellow cheese, my other dairy products were infinitesimal, and my red wine consumption was hardly world class at 12 ounces a day or less, and frequently it was nothing at all.

Then, I read through a hair analysis I'd asked for to give me some indication of trace mineral deficiency or sufficiency. The hair analysis confirmed the sublingual readings about magnesium and potassium deficiency, and it also suggested two other major mineral deficiencies in **manganese** and **zinc**. All of these mineral deficiencies have been demonstrated to accompany and cause nerve disorders, hormonal disorders, neurotransmitter disorders, and very importantly to me, immune system weakness. It was exactly what Jethro Kloss said long ago in the 1930s: mineral deficiencies cause nerve disease and just about everything else. That I had expected.

I had no sense of what trace mineral levels should have been, and to date, have been unable to locate any research which indicates what proper trace minerals levels should be. However, something very suggestive did turn up from the hair analysis. All trace minerals levels were very very low indeed, and one of them, among others, was a low level of molybdenum in my system. I do have an opinion of what should be done and how, though.

99

It would seem obvious that proper levels of trace minerals would be suggested by averaging the findings of trace minerals in a population of healthy individuals, healthy being defined as individuals not being subject to common childhood illnesses or prone to colds and flu, not subject to chronic debilitating conditions, but instead, vibrant energetic people with a medical or life history of not missing work days at their place of employment.

What I had not expected from the mineral analysis was an elevated reading of copper in my hair analysis. It was one of two metals that were off the scale. I had an excess of copper and phosphorus. Schmitt explained copper this way: excessive copper accompanies Candida poisoning. Why? My suspicion is this: copper may be a mineral by-product of yeast metabolism or one of the principal mineral constituents of acetaldehyde. As a kind of pre-vinegar, it may taste like vinegar. At least to my subjective sense of things, vinegars taste like they have copper in them. But that doesn't matter. What matters is that molybdenum chelates out excessive copper from your system sometimes taking the form of a rash on the face or chest. Excessive copper can be just as harmful as a copper deficiency. Mineral deficiencies are the normal problem, and Candida is responsible for disrupting mineral metabolism generally, up and down. It is my guess that molybdenum plays a regulating function, altering levels of other minerals in the same way that magnesium is believed to function, as a regulator of other minerals.

Also unexpected was that all trace minerals analyzed in my hair were interpreted as deficient: **molybdenum**, **vanadium**, **selenium**, and **chromium**. In Dr. Treinen's work, these minerals are a basic part of his Candida treatment.

Fascinatingly, Edgar Cayce said the same kind of thing about Multiple Sclerosis. According to Cayce, one heavy metal deficiency was responsible for MS: a **gold** deficiency. That is surprising in itself since gold has yet to be studied as a required trace mineral or metal. Hey, the big and small pharmaceutical companies could be responsible for raising the price of bullion if they ever start investigating that one. So could all the other smaller companies. It could just be that the fancy French restaurants that serve desserts with gold leaf on them are doing a little more than tickling the fancy of the eyes. They may be providing an essential nutrient at substantial trouble and expense. Maybe the rich know something we don't know.

What is more provocative to me is this: Edgar Cayce, most renowned psychic in the world, claimed that the gold mineral deficiency was caused by "digestive imbalance."

He unfortunately was unable to specify what kind of digestive imbalance.

I know what that is. Candida, CANDIDA, Candida, Candida. Candida causes digestive upset: heartburn, gas, bloating, growling, inability to assimilate minerals and other nutrients, diarrhea, constipation, and finally hemorrhoids. It causes dizziness. I had that symptom too. I tasted something metallic on the back of my tongue, like I had swallowed a copper penny. I had detected that taste since I was as young as 13 and before, before and after the acute phase of infectious polio. I had detected bad odors on my tongue. I also noticed that the sweating I did on my back, and subsequently one night in bed after molybdenum, had a very foul odor to it. I suspect those odors have much to do with acetaldehyde or acetic acid being excreted through the pores of the skin. The youth I had been with a cast iron stomach who could and did eat anything had suddenly developed allergies to nearly all foods when I was later diagnosed for post polio syndrome, almost a universal food reactor. I also developed chronic sinus congestion that came on at night. I had not connected it with Candida. I had acne, pimples, and the clumsiness of adolescence at 51 years of age. I had all of those symptoms, Candida infection symptoms, a diagnosed Candida infection, and a mineral analysis that proved the mineral-deficiency and copper toxic-excess consequences normally accompanying Candida colonization.

But most importantly, Dr. William Crook's *The Yeast Connection* convincingly demonstrated that Candida raised hell with mineral metabolism which in turn can lead to more serious things. This must have been the cause of "digestive imbalance" that Cayce was aware of and had read in the Book of Life. Candida is a known cause of mineral deficiencies. I have Candida; Candida causes mineral deficiencies; I have mineral deficiencies; mineral deficiencies cause nerve disorders.

I decided to take other dietary measures to "manage" Candida, actually a kind of birth control program to reduce the colony's population rather than to declare fungicidal nuclear war on the critters. And I started taking **oil of oregano** because of another fateful encounter with another sales representative, who once again, appeared miraculously at Dr. Cooper's office with a little untranslated German clinical study in his hand.

I think it would make common sense for nearly everyone to add acidophilus to their diets either as a supplement or food simply because every infant tests positive for Candida who has not been breast fed. Human breast milk is said to be rich in **L. acidophilus**. Ordinary cow and goat milk is not, unless it is added to it. Cows may need this acidophilus diet just as much as humans do if not more since they are, in part, responsible for gassing up the universe with methane.

The length of colonization that an infantile infection implies for nearly everyone in the United States, both calves and children, may just account for every known disease and disorder in the civilized, cooked and processed food world including the greenhouse effect. As well as the absence of living acidophilus in food, cooked food of all kinds or overly cooked food in food processing of canned and frozen foods encourages the growth of Candida albicans. Candida thrives on heat processed oils, hydrogenated fats, and sugars. Antibiotics in the meats we consume encourage Candida infection. Antibiotics are the common cause of setting up Candida infection when they are taken as medication or when they are consumed in the foods we eat.

The first case of MS was diagnosed in 1823, approximately ten years after canned food was invented by Napoleon to feed his armies. Drs. R. U. Schwyzer and Hugo Henzi in Switzerland found a high correlation between sugar intake and incidence of Multiple Sclerosis. Two deficiencies went along with it: B12 pernicious anemia and a deficiency in folic acid. Although they blamed sugar in high pectin fruits and in candy for these problems, the more obvious source of the difficulty that they overlooked was food processing itself. **Sugar** in one form or another is commonly used in food processing to enhance flavor or improve texture. You can't even buy tomato sauce in a can without buying added sugar. The result that the Swiss doctors found was that there were high levels of methanol in the blood streams of MS patients, and methanol's byproduct, **formaldehyde**, was apparently found in the damaged myelin sheaths of MS people. This they blamed on fruit pectin and sugar. I would blame it on two other things: another strain of methane producing Candida or methane producing bacteria, the same bacteria that plague the cattle industry. It is commonly assumed that methane producing bacteria are responsible for two things in cattle: enormous and wasteful conversion of feed into methane gas, and cattle are accused of being largely responsible for the greenhouse effect.

There is a much simpler explanation that needs to be investigated in both. Cattle are now commonly fed antibiotics in their feed or injected with them. Antibiotics normally clean out all bacteria, good and bad. If they clean out all bacteria, then methane producing bacteria could not be responsible for methane production. They would have been killed by the antibiotics in their feed. However, fungus and yeasts are unaffected by antibiotics. It is my guess that the same things that set people up for Candida infection also set up cattle for gassing up the universe. If I am right, cattle should not be fed antibiotics at all. They should be fed freeze dried acidophilus in their normal feed for several reasons: it would act as a more effective antibiotic against methane producing bacteria if they are indeed responsible since acidophilus is at once antiviral, antibacterial, and antifungal without harming the friendly bacteria; but more importantly, it would reduce the incidence of alcohol producing yeasts in their systems, whether it be a strain of methanol producing yeast, or ethanol producing yeast. It is also cheaper than synthetic antibiotics.

It would be easily possible to reduce the Candida population by acidophilus capsules, acidophilus milk, kefir, and yogurt as a normal dietary principle for humans as well. For one thing, acidophilus competes in the intestinal tract or anywhere else; it eats up what Candida would have eaten. And if Dr. Bruce McFarland is correct, acidophilus actually feeds Candida properly. That is, the implication is that well fed microbes are not pathogenic, but necessary innocuous and even helpful inhabitants of our bodies.

102

The anti-germ hypothesis of Dr. Richard Murray has always suggested the same thing. Germs are not problems any more than people are when they are well fed. People, immune cells, and germs become stupid when they aren't treated right.

Acidophilus does not gobble up Candida itself. It is not a fungicidal poison or cannibal. Instead, it competes for the available food supply and may even play a cooperative role in keeping other microbes happy and well.

If you have Candida dominance, Candida starves your system. If you have acidophilus in addition, acidophilus balances and nourishes your system. Acidophilus aids proper digestion and digestive balance; Candida imbalance damages normal digestion. We could have healthier cattle, healthier microbes, healthier immune cells, and healthier humans. What is more, acidophilus produces acetic acid and benzoic acid, both of which are unfavorable to unfriendly bacterial forms. Like the hypha of Candida, the little hooks that bacteria use to invade our cells or siphon off our cellular nutrients cannot find a place to hold onto in acidic environments. Acidic environments are a kind of Teflon as described in *The Food Pharmacy*: the surface is so slippery that unfriendly critters slip right on out to Candida heaven and live happily ever after in the sewer system or the fields. Some no doubt continue to live in us, but I believe peacefully, in a peaceful and acceptable coexistence without greenhousing us around, turning us into gas blimps, or undiscovered sources of natural gas.

In fact, I also believe that Candida in moderation also is beneficial to humans as their host. Candida produces alcohol for one thing, and alcohol may be the source of a moderate disinfectant within our intestines and other cells. Alcohol is also a free radical scavenger. The French scientists, not to mention the French wine makers, have always known these things. Read *Wine is the Best Medicine* and see what you think. Read the Blue Cross studies that correlate moderate alcohol consumption with low incidence of heart and artery disease and begin to wonder. Read *The Food Pharmacy* about the beneficial effects of moderate wine and beer consumption and stop feeling guilty for having a drink now and then. The modern puritanical mentality in some health circles needs to be revised. It may be of some interest to you that the average Puritan of our hallowed past drank eight pints of Puritan ale and a half bottle of wine for dinner. Do you remember any complaints about chronic illness mentioned by George Washington? It may be time for Seagram's and our wine makers to seek FDA approval of wine and beer and other beverages as health foods. Imagine reading on a wine bottle that it was good for you in moderation and quoting the French and European studies that support that claim. The latter-day Puritans may not like it, but the alcohol industry and all those who feel like creeps when they have a glass now and then are going to think a lot better of themselves. Of course, alcohol has always been one of the basic invisible ingredients in medicine with equal or greater effects than the medicine itself.

Imagine a world that emphasizes the positive things. It has been clinically demonstrated that grief and depression lower antibody count.

Will someone please start counting the antibodies of people who are positive and happy? We really should be putting humans in our laboratories who know how to stay well. Bring them in for an afternoon cocktail and count their antibodies. Make the environment pleasant, soft music, good talk, invigorate them with good ideas.

Acidophilus also produces acidophilin, a natural "antibiotic" stronger than all the mycin drugs and totally friendly to healthy tissue, according to one Merck scientist quoted somewhat sheepishly in *The Food Pharmacy*. He seemed embarrassed to reveal that a food could do more than all the drug companies combined. It seems they are effective, but not killers, not cannibals, not terrorists. I suspect it is because all of these food substances communicate just as ants communicate, by pheromones, by the equivalent of formic acid, or defensive aromas, or food sharing chemical communication. Bees do the same thing. What we know about insects I believe applies to what we should know about virus, bacteria, and fungal yeasts. All life communicates in the same way. What I want to know is what is acidophilin saying to a yeast or a bacteria? What is marigold or calendula saying to a bug interested in feasting on your tomatoes? What does garlic say to a virus? Are friendly microbes Greeks, Italians, and Cambodians in food ritual chemical communication? I believe they are. Ever noticed that SOME people shy away from others with garlic breath? Guess what, I believe our little brothers and sisters the mites and microbes are just like some of us people are. They shy, pine, and mope in the presence of garlic-breath food environments and get up and leave the area. It depresses them and they sit in the corner so long, some of them die of depression. Some of them run for the sewers, and others metamorphose into friendly, non-pathogenic forms.

Fight or flight, depressant or stimulant, the basic binary code of our cellular, hormonal, and neurotransmitter life, probably operates electrically and chemically on our parasites just as it does in our cellular and insect worlds. Our parasites are part of us. To kill them is to kill ourselves. When a white blood cell digests a parasite, it confers immunity from the parasite. When a parasite is partly attacked by a fungicide or an antibiotic, our white blood cells remember both the parasite and the antibiotic. The next time the synthetic antibiotic comes into our systems, our immune cells remember what they have eaten except that what they have eaten has been confused with the enemy alien, the old parasite, the old flu germ, or whatever. Allergic reactions are common when this kind of confusion takes place.

Internal environmental engineering and sensitivity are different ways of handling the same problem. Most importantly, acidophilus produces your own hydrogen peroxide factory in your gut. Hydrogen peroxide oxygenates your intestines which is critical for one basic thing: pathogenic

Candida has to have an anaerobic environment to live. So do most unfriendly viruses and bacteria. Pathogenic Candida cannot live in oxygen environments. I can't help it if the beasties do not prefer this environment. We all have a right to chose our place. Some of us even choose to become friendly when we have enough "breathing" room.

It's too bad that acidophilus doesn't produce light as well. Candida, virus, and bacteria love the darkness and the dark places of one's body. But I'm sure there is a reason for it. As one very wise post polio person said, "We should smile more often." Her point was in response to a talk I gave at a post polio support group. I said, Candida doesn't like sunlight, and I had been opening my mouth to the sunlight. Smiling may be not only good for your mental health, it may be just as good for chasing away a few bugs in your mouth.

The implications for using light in dentistry are staggering. Imagine a dentist with his sonic torture device for cleaning the plaque off your teeth equipped with a little black light or full spectrum beam. Certainly, it is worth research. Any microbiology lab has light flooding the area to "sterilize" it and prevent contagion. The obvious clinical and self-help implications are incredibly provocative. Of course, these things appeared in medical journals in 1906 but apparently no one paid them any attention.

I had wondered if you just opened your mouth to the sun a little, or yawned around light bulbs if the buggers would die of sun stoke or decide it is vacation-migration time to the dark places of the underworld. Many friendly bacteria may not be able to survive in daylight either which would be the bad news. But I think light experiments *in vitro* would be very easy and satisfying to demonstrate. Our microbiology laboratories are flooded with light, and I know why. What I don't know is whether the clinicians are aware of one of the first photographer's experience with light and microscopic life, John Ott's, good old Walt Disney's chief photographer for the World of Nature. John Ott found that manipulating light on his slides of living cells, which he was photographing, responded in all kinds of different ways to light, light filters, black light, and full spectrum light. He also found that healthy cells died under slides made of glass, but not under slides made of plastic simply because the glass filtered out minute ranges of the spectrum and plastic did not. I'd like to see the research laboratories kept busy in this country on light experiments for the next three centuries.

It seems that the light used in decontamination areas for sterilizing things has an obvious clinical application that has been staring scientists in the face for decades. Light itself discourages pathogens, both viral and bacterial. What exact ranges of the electromagnetic spectrum do exactly what to the metabolism, replication cycles, the life and pursuit of happiness, of pathogens? Would not light be a way of reducing the spiraling of medical costs that all politicians are concerned with, not to mention all the individuals and insurance companies which have to pay the bills?

105

I'd also like to see them busy for four centuries using their spectroscopy instruments on pheromones in flowers, plants, trees, especially garlic and other herbs with intense aromatic properties. Everyone knows that insects are attracted to white incandescent light. Do bugs mistake light for flowers? Does part of the spectrum have an aroma property? It is well known that bees use the polarizing geometry of daylight to map their ways to pollen sources. What I'd like to know is this: is the geometry of polarization perceived as light to a bee, or is it a landscape of aroma, a smell-map which bees sprinkle with pheromones? Fragrances keep mosquitoes off one's skin, and the B vitamins have been known to repel insects. Fascinatingly to me, B vitamins under spectroscopy are known to have yellow orange colors, the very colors that marigolds have, which every organic gardener knows are useful in keeping crop insects out of the gardener's food supply.

I'd like to see the results of the other end of the electromagnetic spectrum explored in the same way. I know what beneficial effects music has on plants and learning. Accelerated-Suggestopedic methods have demonstrated both health and mental functioning enhancement upwards of ten percent. But exactly how does that work? Five centuries of work should tell you the answers on virus, bacteria, fungal yeasts, the cells of rabbit eyes, cellular metabolism of all plants, molds. Will rock music do them in; are bugs classical music enthusiasts; what of our immune system cells; what do they "prefer"? To what tunes does a T-Cell dance? What music puts us to sleep? What musical properties put pathogens to sleep? The work of Ohno in Japan may suggest many starting points. His findings demonstrate that all cellular life encodes music. What if we turned up the volume, turned down the volume, added one note not in the cell's scale?

Taking natural or drug fungicides like the prescription drugs nystatin or nizoral, natural broadspectrum antifungal-antibacterial, antiviral food substances like raw or Kyolic garlic or oil of oregano are choices. If you want to declare war on your internal mites and nuke the bugs, choose the synthetic stuff. If you want to negotiate the politics of your health, choose oregano or garlic or acidophilus, or all three. I chose all three and one more that Egyptians had great success with.

One fascinating German study, still untranslated from the original German, indicated that oil of oregano reduced Candida populations 77%, and that high percentage was without an anti-Candida discouraging diet. Think of how effective it might be if you didn't feed Candida sugar, vinegar, yeast, mushrooms, hydrogenated fats, and refined carbohydrates. Pathogenic Candida is a processed food junky.

If you want to try the ancient Egyptian method of discouraging bugs, you might try **cinnamon**. If you think that a 77% success rate outclasses synthetic drugs, cinnamon does 20 to 22 percentage points better than that: powdered cinnamon is 97 to 99% percent effective in discouraging fungus, bacteria, and virus *in vitro*. It is no wonder that Egyptian mummies have lasted 5,000 years or so. The bugs apparently don't like the smell or the taste of cinnamon mummies. They don't like the taste of Thai food either; cinnamon is a natural food preservative as well. I used cinnamon and acidophilus for brushing my teeth for six months; and when I returned to my dentist, he wanted to know "how I did it." I had had some pretty sick looking gums for years, and suddenly they were healthy and pink looking.

"How did you do that?" my dentist asked.

"Will you take my secret and participate in a little ADA study, write it up, and show how others might prevent tooth decay and gum disease?"

"Of course not," he said.

He refused, so he's not going to know until he reads this book, if he reads this book. Apparently dentistry has been overlooking an obvious cause of tooth decay and gum disease. They have counted the odd bugs, but the ones that are everywhere have been, of course, invisible. Candida is ubiquitous.

Considering President Bill Clinton's interest in reducing the alarming rise of health care costs in the United States, and considering Vice President Al Gore's sensitivity for our environment, I want to make this request of them both. Support Orrin Hatch's Health Freedom Act in the Senate. We as a nation have fewer and fewer choices in the matters that affect us as citizens and individuals. As citizens, we no longer have referendum power in matters of the national budget. We don't get to vote on the Stealth budget, the military budget, the salaries of Senators and Congressmen, or any of the entitlement programs. We have no choices there.

We do have choices in buying or not buying natural foods and food supplements, but this too is threatened by expanded regulatory powers of HR 3642 sponsored by Henry Waxman and Joseph Kennedy. The effects seem to be these: dangerous drugs have no warning labels on them, but harmless food substances may be banned. This makes no sense whatsoever, but may make much sense to the composition of the Advisory Panels of the FDA. These Advisory Panels, as reported in *Investor's Business Daily*, by Christine Shenot, dictate the fates of big and small growth companies alike by their yawns, their smiles, and their groans. It has been that way since 1906. I don't dispute their powers or their veracity in making their determinations. I think we all do the best we can. What I do find troubling is that ALL American interests are not fairly represented on these panels. Does it not make both common sense and constitutional sense that checks and balances exist on these panels? That is, it would be only fair and equitable to have the small growth industries, the organic farmers, the organic dairies, the organic meat producers, the health food industries who produce new products and those who sell them in the stores, homeopaths, naturopaths, acupuncturists, chiropractors, and consumer and consumer advocate groups represented on these panels. There are only two consumer representatives on all of the Advisory Panels, and they have no voting power. There are many M.D.s on the advisory panels, but there are no

107

chiropractors, no homeopaths, no naturopaths, no physical therapists, no physiatrists, and no counselors on these panels. If there were, our choices would be expanded as professionals and consumers, our labeling of products would be more extensive both pro and con, and our costs in health care would be considerably reduced.

Obvious built-in checks and balances would come out of this simple change in the composition of the FDA advisory panels. These panels not only dictate what choices doctors, patients, and consumers have, but they also dictate Wall Street, the rise and fall of companies just trying to start up, and those who are in fact growing. The TASK force idea has evolved in industry to make committees composed of all those levels of persons affected from management to scientist to consumer on such committees. Some of our older institutions have not evolved in that common sense direction.

The practice of health needs such TASK force instruments on their advisory boards. It has yet to occur to the FDA that they are supposed to protect the consumer as well as big industry. The International Polio Network, for one organization, has noted the emergence of many Self-Help groups. Why did these groups emerge and why did they need to emerge at all? The answer is staring us in the face. Too many physicians have forgotten that their mission is to serve the health of the patient. Too many physicians have forgotten that the patient has rights, dignity, and responsibility in making choices for or against health. These groups have emerged because these individuals with chronic conditions were not received well by doctors who were insensitive to their patients' needs and observations, and uninformed about the range of choices that might have helped get them well.

These choices do exist in Europe, in Britain, in China, in Russia, in Japan. They have learned much from us. What have we learned from them? Most of the useful information in this book came from research conducted in foreign countries. Some of it was published in the United States. The result is I know about it, but much more needs to be done in translation and original research.

We need to research and publish infinitely more avenues of inquiry in health. We need to study what works to keep people healthy as well as what works to treat illness. Simple essential trace mineral studies are in their infancy.

Molybdenum may potentially have a vast effect on improving the health of post polio survivors and many other chronic conditions. But clinical studies with nutrients are rare because of fears of the FDA showing up with flak vests and automatic weapons. Physicians can get into trouble presently for conducting such studies because of FDA biases against alternative heath care; however, self-help groups could perform their own for these reasons. Nutrients are not drugs, nor should they be defined that way. A self-help group could study information and empower itself to do whatever it chooses. As far as I know, the FDA may not restrict an individual's freedom of choice even though it has exercised that power over physicians. The FDA cannot abridge an individual's constitutional rights. But the FDA may abridge the constitutional rights of the health professions. So it is my guess, that self-empowered food supplement studies should be conducted by self-help groups. I believe them to be the future of where discoveries are to be made. Institutions move very slowly.

Molybdenum may have an obvious application to treatment of alcoholism, but that kind of clinical study is yet to be done also. Molybdenum may have an obvious application to Chronic Fatigue Syndrome, Lupus, Multiple Sclerosis, Alzheimer's disease, Parkinson's disease, but that research has yet to be conducted. Support Groups for Chronic Illness exist all over the United States and daily discuss potentially rich research ideas on electronic bulletin boards.

Selenium, vanadium, chromium, and **germanium** are also recognized essential trace minerals in human nutrition. What studies are being conducted to find out what illnesses or conditions they might help, and what studies are being conducted to find out what roles they play in health? Japan is way ahead of us in knowing about germanium and how it works to assist prescription medication.

There have been 72 to 119 trace minerals identified. What role does gold play in human nutrition? It is one of the 119. What role does silver play? It is one of the 119. Does the wearing of jewelry made of silver and gold play a role in the topical absorption of those trace mineral-metals? Is this why copper bracelets work in some arthritic conditions? Would the jewelry industry be interested in cooperating with the FDA in finding out? Or would the FDA like to regulate the jewelers too? Would Wall Street be interested in the implications for commodity prices?

More important than any of this is that we may be able to create a new cooperative ethic: all phases of health care should be available to patients, located in one building like a health-care task force, with industry, professional scientist, chiropractor, M.D., masseuse, masseur, acupuncturist, homeopath, naturopath, together in one place, in hospitals, in office buildings, to finally share information, share approaches, and offer patients the right to choose among apparently competing approaches which I believe to be complementary. We would reduce rental costs, energy costs, research costs, and the most important cost of all—the cost of poor health, debility, and disease. We could do it cheaper, and we could do it better.

What is more, we need to feed the people who are starving. We need to do that for spiritual reasons, for humanitarian reasons and for our own economic survival. But equally important, we need to feed ourselves. We can do it with improved natural supplements of food, natural vitamins, minerals, and supplements, or we can invite the good German, Japanese, British, Russian, and other pharmaceutical Peace Corps to come to the United States and do it for us. I know what the balance of trade is. We should take advantage of our junior growth health care industry, encourage it, not kill it, and do it before it is done for us.

Equally important, fair and equal representation should be present on FDA advisory committees which regulate foods, food additives, and drugs. It is a surprise to me that warning labels have not appeared that warn consumers of irradiation of foods and neurotoxins in vaccines, but warning labels do appear on alcohol and cigarettes. It is a surprise to me that Philip Morris does not have a counter label that claims that smoking in moderation may be good for you. It was after all used as a treatment for disease by the ancient Egyptians. They smoked illness away.

I suspect the answer is obvious enough. The tobacco industry does not sit on the advisory committees, the French scientists who know that wine is good for you in moderation do not sit on the FDA committees, the wine making industry and all other alcohol beverage industries must not sit on advisory committees, the health food industries must not be a part of the committees, the small growth industries that produce vitamins and minerals must not be on the committees, the 13 organic dairy farmers in Wisconsin must not be represented on the committee, homeopaths must not be represented, naturopaths must not be represented, and consumers must not be represented who are interested in preserving the choices that may be preserved by Orrin Hatch's Health Freedom Bill before the Senate.

It would seem to me that one phone call from President Clinton to whoever appoints the constituency of such FDA advisory committees might in five minutes make for a fair, equitable, and balanced committee and considerably lower the costs of many alternative health care approaches. I know what Teddy Roosevelt's call to the Secretary of Agriculture did for Dr. Harvey Wiley. President Roosevelt overturned the Food and Drug Act of 1906 in the same year of its creation by asking the bureaucracy to act as a friend of industry, not a friend of the consumer. Read Dr. Harvey W. Wiley, M.D., *The History of a Crime Against the Food Law: The Amazing Story of the National Food and Drugs Law Intended to Protect the Health of the People, Perverted to Protect the Adulteration of Foods and Drugs* (1929). Phone calls accomplish amazing things.

Another phone call from Hillary Clinton might just do a lot of good if she where to place such a call to all insurance companies. It seems that insurance companies receive such "calls" from the AMA and the ADA and the APA. These organizations lobby not only presidents and congress but insurance companies. It seems very unfortunate that chiropractors, naturopaths, masseuses and masseurs, acupuncturists, the AARP, all organizations that support alternative medicine don't seem to be able to make such "calls" on their own. There are great numbers of individuals who have discovered that a $40 chiropractic treatment costs much less than a $30,000 operation. In fact there are others paying $6,000 to $12,000 a year for AZT who might want to pay a little less for nutritional alternatives, massage, and acupuncture. I'd say a fair guess would be that $500 or less might favorably compete in cost from alternative health care practitioners, the insurance companies might have slightly more money in their coffers, and the AIDS patients might even get better for much less money.

Those who read the *Wall Street Journal* article on the Chinese curing AIDS with cucumbers might want to add up and compare the cost of a hundred cucumbers to AZT. Even Magic Johnson might be interested in adding a few cucumbers to his diet, or perhaps flying to China and being treated and cured there. Of course, cucumber treatment is unavailable in the United States. Should we fly all the AIDS patients to China and let their doctors make that income, or should we be importing a little more information and a few less cars?

I don't suppose it has occurred to the insular mentality of the pharmaceutical companies to hire a few Russian, Chinese, Japanese, German, and British scientists who know how to do things cheaply. I don't suppose it will ever occur to them. You see, we can't export our expensive wonder drugs to either China or Russia because they can't afford wonder drug prices. It also seems that some of the rest of us recession-bound individuals can't always afford them either.

Chapter 11

MOLYBDENUM:
Recycling Fatigue into Energy

A Self-Help Study Showing the Results of 31 People with Chronic Illness Taking Molybdenum for 30 Days (published in *Townsend Letter for Doctors*, April 1994; *The Digest of Chiropractic Economics*, May June, 1994).

- Since I felt that Molybdenum was the chief player in turning around my own chronic illness, I wanted to test out just how well it would work for others with chronic illness (Chronic Fatigue Syndrome, Lupus, Arthritis, Post Polio Syndrome, & undiagnosed symptoms)
- I found 31 people subject to chronic illness who agreed to take molybdenum for 30 days to determine its effects on:
- Chronic Fatigue—65% reported improved energy levels
- General Weakness—68% reported improvements in strength
- Joint Pain—61% reported lesser pain
- Muscle Pain—61% reported less muscle pain
- Headaches—55% reported fewer headaches
- Concentration—65% reported improved concentration
- Memory—71% reported improvements in the ability to remember
- Depression—55% reported improvements
- Insomnia—61% reported improved sleeping patterns

At least a decade's worth of personal experimentation had led me to find answers to my own chronic illness involving chronic fatigue, extreme muscular weakness, generalized pain, insomnia, and other disgusting things. The causes had been variously diagnosed as mononucleosis or Epstein-Barr virus, poor health caused by lack of exercise, lupus, psychosomatic illness, depression, slow pertussis infection, post polio syndrome, allergies, chronic fatigue, faulty brain chemistry, and Candida albicans infection.

The chief player in resolving my problems was an essential trace mineral, molybdenum. With molybdenum, it was possible to transform poisons into energy.

In trying to "kill" a massive Candida colonialization in my GI track, my mouth, and toenails, I made discoveries. The antibiotic nystatin had made all of my symptoms worse. First, it must have been responsible for attacking and killing vast numbers of the fungal yeast, candida; and as Orian Truss, *The Missing Diagnosis*, and William Crook, *The Yeast Connection*, had said, large doses of antibiotics can make an "unpleasant condition" worse. Their hypothesis was that the yeast "byproducts" from the kill-off were responsible for sites remote from the infection being affected.

Neither Dr. Truss nor Dr. Crook were aware of how the garbage from yeast actually affected the body or the brain. They only knew that sites remote from the infection were affected: the brain, the central nervous system, the joints, the muscles. In 1984, Dr. Truss suspected aldehydes caused the problems, but was unable to suggest a way of getting rid of them. The normal solution has been to kill the parasite that produced the aldehyde, and not to bother with the parasite's garbage by-products.

In experiencing the effects of the "kill-off," I began to have definite feelings that killing the yeast was wrong. That is how we as a culture respond to anything we don't understand. Ethically speaking, we consider strangers enemies. We go to war with anything that is different. War itself on a political level causes untold human suffering, and the aftermath may be the worst of all. The emotional and economic garbage of war persists for centuries. The debts of the American Civil War are still unpaid. If we learn to cooperate with the strangers on our borders, we would have a different world. If we learned how to treat microbes strange to the human body as guests of the body, we might just discover health.

Molybdenum is one way of cleaning up the garbage of our antibiotic wars. Candida albicans is a normal inhabitant of our gastrointestinal tract. It is supposed to be there. And if Dr. Bruce McFarland is correct, it causes no problem when it is fed well and treated well. When does it cause a problem?

Half of the problem is created by modern medical wonder drugs: the birth control pill which alters the hormone system and subsequently the immune system, antibiotics, steroids, and other chemotherapies which are synthetic ways of altering the function of the body's systems, wiping out the ecosystem in the stomach and gut, and setting up a scenario for trouble. As friendly E. coli, L. bifidus, L. bulgaricus, L. acidophilus bacteria are killed by the use of prescription drugs right along with the alien microbes, candida fungal yeasts begin to flourish and dominate, growing to such numbers that they may outnumber every cell in the human body.

Two basic events take place. Our friendly bacteria no longer aid digestion by converting food into enzymes, amino acids, vitamins, and minerals that the body can use; so killing sets us up for subclinical and clinical malnutrition syndromes.

The other half of the problem is industrialized, overly processed, heat processed or chemically processed foods. Candida and herpes zoster, for two, are junk food junkies thriving on **refined sugar, processed vegetable**

114

oils, and **hydrogenated fats**. None of these "foods" are found in nature. So how does the body respond to hydrogenated fats? One result is that candida digests a part of them into pseudo bile. Pseudo bile tells your appetite center that the fat is taken care of, and you need more. So you develop cravings for more junk as undigested fat collects in the body. Undigested fat collects in the arteries too, and you may get artery and heart problems. Another problem of incomplete digestion results in food substances going into the blood that shouldn't be there. Methionine becomes homocysteine rather than glutamine and taurine. We are not allergic to foods; we are allergic to incompletely digested foods.

Candida also converts sugars into ethanol. Ethanol is not bad in itself. It functions as a free radical scavenger and antiseptic. It provides a janitorial function for the body. But too much unused alcohol converts into aldehydes. If you have adequate amounts of **glutamine, magnesium, manganese, selenium, niacin, folic acid, B6, B12, iron**, and **molybdenum**, aldehydes continue to be metabolized into acetic acid, which can be excreted, or converted further into acetyl coenzyme A. If these nutrients are in poor supply, aldehydes begin collecting in the body's tissues.

So when candida is fully nourished or we are, candida furnishes the body with a necessary part of the Krebs energy cycle necessary for the health and maintenance of all cells. When our digestion is unbalanced, we incompletely convert sugars into poisons and they stay poisons in our human systems. When our digestion is balanced, or we give it what it needs in terms of supplements, a potential poison is transformed into a source of energy: aldehyde poison becomes acetyl coenzyme A.

Why should we love our enemies? Because our enemies are ourselves. The enemy candida, and it is an enemy in Drs. Truss's and Crook's eyes, and in the eyes of most of the medical profession, is our friend or becomes our friend when we treat it right. If we attack it with antibiotics, the rest of our friendly microbes will be unable to feed it the B vitamins, amino acids, and minerals it needs to metabolize its poisons into nourishment for our bodies. When we attack our microbes, we kill ourselves.

Within days of taking 100 mcg of molybdenum three times a day, I could feel the poisons from candida garbage transforming themselves into heat and energy. Where I had experienced pain in my neck and shoulders, I felt warmth. A stiff back that felt like a wall of steel was transformed into copious sweat. My muscles relaxed and were pain free. At the same time, the person I was who found it difficult to get out of bed, became someone who needed 4 to 8 hours of sleep rather than 10 or 12. Where I had been confined within a prison of fatigue, the fatigue was translated into an open expanse of energy and possibility. An intellectual fog that had filled my head for years scattered itself the first day I took molybdenum. I had lived with an aldehyde hangover for so long, I had no idea what it was like to experience mental clarity.

I designed a Self-Help Molybdenum study, consumer oriented, that was not medically or company sponsored. People simply chose to participate or not participate, without medical diagnosis or advice.

In reading histories of placebo treatments, it became obvious to me that "scientific" studies attempted to avoid placebo effects that, on average, reported a 36% rate of effectiveness, slightly greater effectiveness than with the "real thing" prescription medication it would be pared against. Typical of some studies was the bemoaning of the fact that placebo effects were not maximized. That is, health professionals who had the best interests of the patients in mind wanted to use positive suggestion in addition to the medication. However, few if any of such professionals, had the courage to do it. Why? It was unscientific. Wouldn't it be terrible if people got better because of attitude change?

In other readings, it became apparent that lactose, sugar, or olive oil were commonly used as placebos. In view of my modest knowledge of biochemistry, this seemed outrageous to me. Lactose, sugar, and olive oil are all bioactive substances. Lactose, for one, is so little regarded as a nutrient, that it is the most common binder in prescription medication. Yet the *Food Pharmacy* made clear that plain old **sugar** acts as nature's tranquilizer. Dr. Richard Murray had pointed out that **lactose** contains the two essential building blocks, glucose and galactose, of the central nervous system and brain. The body uses supplies of glucose for conversion into N-**acetyl glucosamine** to maintain and repair all of our tissues. **Olive oil** is known to favorably affect good cholesterol, and **good cholesterol** is the nutrient precursor for our hormones, our vitamin D, nerve and brain maintenance and repair, and bile for digesting fats. It seemed no wonder to me that placebo effects could be accounted for not on the basis of expectation alone, but on a biochemical level. To me, this meant that most double or single blind experiments were triple blind. Nutrients like **vitamin B12** and **folic acid** are so little regarded that they have been used as placebos in the treatment of multiple sclerosis. The greatest irony of all was not that placebos may have worked better than the prescription medication, but that the prescription medication may have done some of its good because of the binder hiding inside of it. All of this led me away from the mechanistic attitudes that were behind "scientific credibility."

We are humans who deserve to know what the hopes are of those who intend to help us. We are not chemical machines. So I decided to declare what I knew about molybdenum, what effects had been noticed by Walter Schmitt, Jr., D.C., in "Molybdenum for Candida albicans patients and other conditions," and what the positive, even miraculous results were that I had experienced. My view was and is that the name of the game is doing what is helpful in as positive and cheerful way as possible. If positive expectation is helpful, use it. So I maximized rather than minimized the so-called placebo effect and wished everyone choosing to participate a similar success.

People choosing to participate filled out a symptom chart before beginning the study, and once again after completing 30 days of chewing or sucking on a 100 mcg tablet three times a day. The people choosing to participate all shared symptoms of chronic illness: chronic fatigue, chronic muscle weakness, joint pain, muscle pain, headaches, concentration problems, memory problems, problems with depression, and insomnia. Participants ranged in age from 36 to 84. The average age was 54, 13 men and 18 women. Of the 31 people who completed the study, 10 were subject to PPS.

Gratifying results took place for about 2/3's of the people who did try the supplement.

Changes in Chronic Fatigue

65% reported improved energy levels

10% reported lower energy levels at the end of the study

25% reported no change

Of those who responded positively or negatively, there was a 28% average gain in energy. The metabolic pathway that diagrams the likely cause is—

ethanol —}aldehyde —}acetic acid —}acetyl coenzyme A.

A toxin, acetaldehyde, can be transformed into a source of energy, acetyl coenzyme A provided there is adequate molybdenum in the diet or through supplement form. One 84-year-old woman had such low energy levels that she simply couldn't get going in the morning. At 10 AM, she had chewed on one tablet, then cleaned her house for the first time in 5 years, went shopping in the afternoon, worked in the garden, and was still going strong late at night. Since she called up one participant on the survey to complain that old women shouldn't have that kind of energy, I then heard about it second hand. She took only 1/4 of a tablet thereafter. Three other participants for similar reasons did the same thing. To me, that was success. For them, I guess they were more comfortable with their customary levels of fatigue. I enjoyed having new energy. Others were frightened by it. Others were disappointed in having less dramatic gains, but most did experience gains.

Changes in Chronic Weakness

68% reported improved strength

10% reported that weakness became worse

22% reported no change in strength

Of those showing a response, a 24% general improvement took place. One 74-year-old woman reported being able to climb stairs that she had been unable to climb after about two weeks of the supplement. Another reported being able to stand up from a seated position without using his arms to push off. Others had less dramatic changes.

Changes in Joint Pain

61% reported slight to dramatic improvements

6% reported getting worse

32% reported no change

One 67-year-old post polio survivor had been disappointed that nothing miraculous had happened during the first two weeks of supplementation. Then, in the third week, she experienced a pleasant "red hot" warmth where she had had intense sharp pain before in her hip. Only two people seemed to notice a rapid change from pain to pleasant heat.

Changes in Muscle Pain

61% reported less pain to being pain free

29% reported no change

10% reported feeling worse

Any detoxification process may result in reruns of old problems. Ten of the people in the study experienced the brief return of old rashes, old allergic responses, itching, acne like redness and pimples on the face, brief recapitulations of ear aches, and migraines. In asking Dr. Schmitt for his explanation of rashes, his opinion was that excessive copper was working itself out of the system, excess copper being one of the normal clinical findings for people with candida infections.

Another theoretical explanation occurred to me. It is known that mercury collects at sites of physical or chemical injury. My feeling was that aldehydes and ammonia may do the same thing just as Dr. R.U. Schwzyer had found with formaldehyde in MS patients. On one level, aldehydes, known as fragrances, may be responsible for giving a chemical signal to foreign microbes or to our own immune system. Aldehydes may suggest that a chemical-decay process is taking place, so that the immune system may rush to the site to clean up the mess. This may account for what Dr. Schmitt has elsewhere called pseudoinfection triggered by free radicals. Providing a mineral that starts a new chemical reaction may reactivate old problems temporarily.

Changes in Headaches

55% of the people reported fewer or lesser headaches

13% reported more headaches

32% reported no change

One 46-year-old woman, who rarely drank red wine because it gave her wanging headaches, reported that a glass of red wine no longer had that effect. Sulfur containing amino acids, sulfites, are used as a preservative in wines, salad bars, and fresh vegetables at grocery stores. Molybdenum, as Dr. Schmitt has pointed out, helps convert potentially harmful sulfites into taurine, a beneficial amino acid. Drs. Chaitow and Treinen have pointed out that glutamine assists in this process, metabolizing toxic accumulations of ammonia, byproducts of our cellular metabolism, and allowing them to be excreted out of our cells. You then have a brain working at a full, healthy capacity.

Changes in Mental Concentration

65% of the participants reported improvements

3% reported getting worse

32% reported no change

Unexpected and unnoticed by me was something very important to four people on the study. All four noticed a kind of emotional clearheadedness in addition to gains in concentration. One of the four said that her feelings were very close to the surface where she could get to them rather than her feelings getting to her. Rather than let a grocery clerk intimidate her, she stood up for herself and the issue was resolved. Two reported an emotional even temperedness where small annoyances were no longer life-and-death threatening situations. Another who feared social interaction reported actually enjoying and looking forward to being with people.

Mark Johnson has said that candida in some unknown way was known to be responsible for all kinds of neurotransmitter disruptions. I have a strong suspicion that aldehydes and ammonia accumulations cause those mental and emotional dysfunctions by fouling the chemical communication process.

Changes in Memory

71% reported improvements in ability to remember

No person reported getting worse

29% reported noticing no change

Autopsies of post polio survivors who died in the 1950's were reexamined by Richard Bruno, Ph.D. Looking at the brain rather than the already noted damage to the myelin and frayed nerve endings to muscles, Dr. Bruno noticed pinholes Swiss-cheesing the hypothalamus. His assumption was that the original polio infection had caused brain damage which was responsible for the post polio syndrome. I suspect that another explanation is more likely. As aldehydes slowly collect in the brain from auto exhaust, carpets, glue, wood amalgams, candida infection and are not metabolized, a fair guess would be that an autoimmune system attack is triggered by the rancidity of the aldehyde smell. A kind of auto-cannibalism may then set up conditions that are later diagnosed as Parkinson's, Alzheimer's, PPS, MS. Of some surprise to Drs. Henzi and Schwzyer of Switzerland was finding formaldehyde in the myelin sheaths of MS survivors. They blamed fruit pectin and candy bars; we could more easily blame the omnipresence of sugar in processed foods encouraging colonization of candida and the side effects of drugs.

The Merck Manual (1993) recognizes dextrose, the most common sugar additive to canned food, as leading to B1 deficiency responsible for polioencephalitis brain lesions (p.967). Sugar converts into aldehydes. The pattern is clear.

Aldehydes are pickling agents. They are responsible for alcohol hangovers after over-indulgence. They are responsible for a tobacco smoker's hangover from excessive smoking. They have also been blamed for the hangover some people experience when they drink diet drinks with aspartame or NutraSweet. Aspartame converts into aldehydes during digestion. When aldehydes irritate muscles, you get a muscle hangover. When aldehydes irritate skin, you get eczema. When they irritate the myelin sheath, you get Multiple Sclerosis. Long-term neurological irritation may lead to Parkinson's, Alzheimer's, Fibromyalgia, Chronic Fatigue Syndrome, Post Polio Syndrome, or many other Motor Neuron Diseases.

The damage noticed in many chronic diseases may just be triggered by unmetabolized aldehydes and ammonia toxicity. Dr. Henzi's success with folic acid and B12 placebos even suggests why. Sulfur containing amino acids become ammonia and remain ammonia without adequate folic acid, B12, glutamine, and molybdenum.

Changes in Depression

55% reported improvement in mood

3% reported a worsening of depression

42% reported no change

Of those responding to molybdenum, an overall 23% improvement was reported in symptoms. One woman who had used Xanax for years during PMS mood swings and pain, reported that she no longer felt the need to use it. One other subject to PMS stress reported absolutely no PMS symptoms during the month she used molybdenum. The PMS connection was a totally unexpected result. Hormone balance must have been favorably affected. Of course, most of the women were beyond the age when that may have been a problem.

Changes in Insomnia

61% reported improved sleeping patterns

10% reported increased insomnia

29% reported no change

Of those responding in this area, an average 20% improvement in sleep was reported. It might be that aldehydes and ammonia toxins foul serotonin, tryptophan, and B6 metabolism. B6 is one of the many forms that serotonin changes into, and B6 is necessary for metabolizing aldehydes. If there were a B6 deficiency, aldehydes would accumulate, and serotonin levels would be impaired, thus causing poor sleep and other neurotransmitter disruptions.

120

Many other studies with chronic conditions, self help and physician sponsored, should be done with molybdenum, selenium, glutamine, chromium, vanadium, B6, folic acid, iron, and B12.

All of the these vitamins and minerals are important in removing toxic accumulations of either aldehydes or ammonia from the body. All play a role in the sugar-aldehyde-acetyl-coenzyme A pathway and have an impact on energy production for the body.

According to the October 1992 *Townsend Letter for Doctors*, chronic pain was associated with deficient levels of vitamins **B2, B6,** and **B12** in 78% of the patients studied. Increasing levels by supplementation also showed reduction of pain in 65% of Maurice Tinterow's patients at the Center for the Improvement of Human Functioning International. The removal of the aldehyde irritant is suggested again.

In a British study reported in 1992, 200 mcg of selenium reduced pain in 6 out of 8 patients in double-blind trials while there was no significant improvement in the placebo groups. Selenium was shown to be an anti-inflammatory, free radical scavenger assisting the natural inflammatory process. **Selenium** also plays a role in the metabolism of irritating aldehydes. In a Swedish study of hard water reported in December 1992, as selenium and other mineral content of water went up, heart disease went down. In proper amounts, *The Well Mind Association* reported that selenium can block mercury, cadmium, and arsenic poisoning. But in excessive amounts, selenium can be responsible for brittle nails, nails with bumps and ridges, and skin sores. In Vilcabamba, Ecuador, water supplies, soil, and vegetables are rich in selenium, chromium, zinc, manganese, potassium, calcium, magnesium, and trace minerals. Even though the Ecuadorians are all tobacco smokers and drinkers of 100 proof booze, they live way beyond 100 years without breast cancer, Alzheimer's, and other debilitating conditions of modern society. Vilcabamba suggests much about mineral sufficiency.

In Britain, University of Southampton researchers were able to reverse Chronic Fatigue Syndrome after finding low **magnesium** levels in red blood cells. In a group of 32 people, 15 received intramuscular injections of magnesium sulfate. Twelve of the 15 had energy scores that went from the minimum to the maximum after receiving extra magnesium. Magnesium is part of the aldehyde pathway and the Krebs energy cycle.

As early as 1915, the French surgeon, Pierre Delbet, found that magnesium chloride cleansed wounds, had a tonic effect on digestion, senile tremors, Parkinson's, muscle cramps, disorders of the nervous system, acne, eczema, psoriasis, warts, hair loss, impotence, and nearly everything else. In one epidemiological study reported in the *Townsend Letter for Doctors*, areas that showed magnesium rich soils also showed low incidence of cancer.

Diet and alcoholism studies are among those that might profit from the trace mineral **molybdenum.**

Four people reported intense craving for sugar at the beginning of the study, but nausea when sugar was consumed towards the end. Excessive candida presence may dictate cravings in diet; reduced candida garbage may alter such cravings, including the craving for alcohol. The same people reported weight loses from 4 to eight pounds, and in two cases, the loss of two inches around the waist and neck. Molybdenum is known to play a role in fat, carbohydrate, and protein metabolism. Molybdenum sufficiency may be a chief player in transforming metabolic toxins in our bodies into sources of restful sleep and vitality at the same time it reduces the waist-line. Rather than strangle in our own environmental and cellular waste, humble nutrients may help us recycle our garbage and turn it into energy for our cells.

References:

Carper, Jean, *The Food Pharmacy*, Bantam, NY,1988.

Chaitow, Leon, D.O., N.D., *Amino Acids in Therapy*, Healing Arts Press, Vermont, 1988.

Challem J, Lewin R, New clues to multiple sclerosis. *Let's Live* January 1993: 66-68.

Mindell, Earl, *Vitamin Bible*, Warner, NY, 1991.

Murray, Richard, D.C., Lactose, Institute of Practical Biochemistry 1: 1, part B.

Schmitt, Walter, Jr., D.C., Molybdenum for candida albicans patients and other problems. *Digest of Chiropractic Economics* 1991; 31: 4:56-63.

Schmitt, Walter, Jr., D.C., The clorox test: a screening device for free radical pathology. *Digest of Chiropractic Economics* 1987; 30:2, 30:3.

Chapter 12

Molybdenum for Candida Albicans Patients and Other Problems

by Walter H. Schmitt, Jr., D.C.

[This article first appeared in *The Digest of Chiropractic Economics*, 31:4, January-February, 1991, pp. 56-63, 29229 Six Mile Road, Livonia, Michigan 48152-3661, Phone: (313) 427-5720, and is reprinted as it appeared with permission of the author and Chiropractic News Publishing, Company, Inc., courtesy of Keith A. Tosolt, Managing Editor.]

ABSTRACT: The essential trace element, molybdenum, (pronounced mo-lib' de-num) is discussed in relation to its various metabolic pathways. Diagnostic approaches for molybdenum include applied kinesiological procedures based on strong muscles weakening when a patient sniffs aldehydes, ammonia, or Clorox, or tastes sulfur-containing amino acids. Other patterns indicating a need for molybdenum are the same as would be seen in a need for iron and/or excess of copper. Each of these metabolic pathways are shown to be important in the problems of the Candida albicans patient, as well as other patients. Protocols for supplementation and natural sources of molybdenum are given.

INTRODUCTION

Molybdenum is an essential trace element in human nutrition which is understood about as well as it is pronounced. In fact, there is no laboratory testing which has been standardized for the evaluation of molybdenum. Although it has been measured in both blood and hair, the normal values for these tests have yet to be established, and although it is accepted as an essential nutrient for humans, there has yet to be a recommended daily allowance or minimum daily requirement officially established. However, its importance in numerous patients, including those with Candida albicans allergy, has been paramount.

Molybdenum has been studied both directly in the blood and hair[1], indirectly by looking at other metabolites which relate to the presence of molybdenum[2,3] and by applied kinesiological (A.K.) analysis by Dr. Richard Mowles[4]. Most of the background for this paper is taken from the above references as well as standard biochemistry texts. However, the work of Mowles has paralleled the work of this author, and we have expanded on his original findings for the bulk of the clinical information in this paper.

Molybdenum is necessary for the function of at least three important enzymes in the body: 1) aldehyde oxidase for our bodies' handling of aldehydes it produces and those encountered in the environment; 2) xanthine oxidase for the conversion of purines into uric acid; and 3) sulfite oxidase for the conversion of irritating sulfites into harmless sulfates. In addition, molybdenum is found in many biological processes in conjunction with iron and is found to cause a response in AK indicators similar to that of iron. Also, molybdenum is an antagonist to copper and vice versa. Considering all of the above factors has led to our understanding of how molybdenum is usually a necessary adjunct in the treatment of Candida albicans allergy patients and has speeded the recovery of most of these patients even above and beyond the effective natural procedures which were described in a previous paper by Mowles and this author.[5]

MOLYBDENUM AND ALDEHYDES

Chemical aldehydes are best known as fragrances. The body also produces various aldehydes as part of its normal metabolic pathways. One pathway in the metabolism of the essential amino acid, threonine, is its conversion into acetaldehyde and then on into acetic acid for eventual production of acetyl coenzyme A (See Figure 1.) Ethanol, or drinking alcohol, is also processed to acetaldehyde. The build-up of aldehydes can be very toxic to the body's tissues. Therefore, the body has an enzyme which breaks down the aldehydes to less toxic substances. This enzyme is aldehyde oxidase, or sometimes, aldehyde dehydrogenase. Aldehydes encountered dietarily or environmentally or produced in the body must be handled by aldehyde oxidase metabolic pathways.

THREONINE → ACETALDEHYDE → ACETIC ACID → ACETYL CoA

Figure 1

Acetaldehyde is a particularly toxic substance which, in addition to being produced from threonine and ethanol, is a product of the metabolism (i.e. fermentation) of carbohydrate in yeast—hence, the Candida connection. Acetaldehyde is thought to be the major source of tissue damage in alcoholics rather than ethanol itself. The conversion of acetaldehyde into acetic acid is shown in Figure 2. Note that this reaction requires NAD (niacinamide) and aldehyde oxidase is dependent on FAD (riboflavin), iron (Fe), and molybdenum (Mo).

124

```
                          FAD
        NAD               Fe                NADH + H
          ↘               Mo                  ↗
ACETALDEHYDE→-----------------------------------→ACETIC ACID
                    ALDEHYDE OXIDASE
```

Figure 2

Candida albicans and any other patients who complain of sensitivities to various fragrances and airborne odors will be found to have a problem with an olfactory challenge with an aldehyde and will be found to be in need of one or more of the nutrients associated with the metabolism of aldehydes, that is niacinamide, riboflavin, iron and/or molybdenum. Mowles[4] had patients sniff a dilute source of formaldehyde and observed the results in muscle testing patients. In 15 patient trials with weakening on smelling formaldehyde, 14 were found to strengthen on molybdenum. Our clinical procedure paralleled that of Mowles, although we used different sources of aldehydes.

Our original investigation involved using nail polish remover (Cutex brand) as a source of acetone. We were attempting to use an olfactory challenge for ketones since transketolase enzyme is vitamin B-1 (thiamine) dependent. We had performed the functional blood test for red blood cell transketolase on a number of patients and found some of them to show a need for vitamin B-1. Knowing that nail polish remover is primarily acetone, we attempted olfactory challenging to observe the results. Eventually, we switched to using pure acetone for olfactory challenging because of the sporadic results we observed from using the nail polish remover.

A close look at the contents of the Cutex bottle revealed that besides acetone, a fragrance and a food color had been added. It is useful here to mention when testing with sniffing acetone, a strengthening of weak muscles or a weakening of strong muscles has been demonstrated to be associated with a need for vitamin B-1. The proper B-1 tablet, either high synthetic doses or low, natural source, or occasionally both, when insalivated, will block the weakening response to sniffing acetone in those patients who show it, and will likewise mimic the strengthening response in that group of patients.

Although we still occasionally use the nail polish remover as a screening test for acetone and B-1 involvement, we now know that many of our original sporadic observations were due to the presence of a fragrance (i.e., an aldehyde) in the product. We obtained a source of benzaldehyde, which is the smell of almonds and quite pleasant. In the meantime, we had communicated with Mowles and found out about his results with formaldehyde. In an effort to find a less offensive odor, we opted for the benzaldehyde. Further searching led to a source of acetaldehyde itself, and that is now our first choice when challenging the aldehyde oxidase activity with olfactory testing.

When we initially screen a patient, we perform several olfactory challenges by having our patients sniff such substances as Clorox,[6] acetone, an aldehyde, and ammonia, which will be discussed later. We observe for strengthening of weak muscles, and especially a weakening of strong muscles. In an aldehyde sensitive patient, there will be a generalized weakening of all of their muscles when they sniff an aldehyde. We have observed some patients who are sensitive to one aldehyde and not to another, and although this is uncommon, it is useful to keep more than one source of pure or diluted pure aldehyde present, for use in ruling out an aldehyde problem in a difficult patient.

When a patient weakens with sniffing an aldehyde, assume a problem with the aldehyde oxidase enzyme system. To further evaluate this pattern, check a muscle or muscles which are weak in the clear using oral insalivation of each of the four substances associated with the metabolism of aldehyde oxidase system: niacinamide, riboflavin, iron, and molybdenum. We usually start with molybdenum because it is the most commonly found fact in our practice.

When molybdenum, or one of the other three substances, strengthens the weak muscles, we then have the patient again sniff the aldehyde with the neutralizing substance in the mouth. Sometimes, one of the nutrients will strengthen a weak muscle but will not negate the aldehyde sniff response. We only supplement the nutrient which both strengthens the weak muscle and negates the weakening response of the aldehyde sniff.

Patients with aldehyde sensitivity will demonstrate a number of symptoms. The most severe cases we have observed are those patients with systemic Candida albicans allergy syndrome. Many of these patients are incredibly sensitive to any type of fragrance. This becomes easily understood in light of the idea that Candida in the G.I. tract, vagina, or elsewhere in the body is giving off acetaldehyde as part of its normal metabolism. The excess stress which this must put on the aldehyde oxidase enzyme systems in the body's tissues leaves them unable to keep up with the extra demand. Supplementation of molybdenum and/or niacinamide, riboflavin, and iron will improve the patient's ability to handle the Candida generated aldehydes, as well as those encountered in the environment.

When an aldehyde sensitivity exists, there is a considerable tissue irritation due to the buildup of these substances. It appears from our clinical observations that some patients fall into a vicious cycle of aldehyde sensitivity where there is a depletion of one or more of the aldehyde oxidase related nutrients which leads to an increase tissue irritation from Candida produced aldehyde. This tissue irritation lowers tissue resistance which sets up vulnerability to future invasion by the Candida albicans or other infectious agents reinitiating the cycle over again. This pattern often accompanies the "pseudoinfection syndrome" previously discussed by this author,[6] and appears to be responsible, at least in part, for many patients with chronic vaginitis from a yeast infection.

We have observed at least one patient who has been plagued with recurrent vaginal yeast infections, at least once monthly, for many years. Every possible allopathic approach has been unsuccessful in controlling the recurrence of these infections. Mycostatin (Nystatin) as vaginal suppositories has been useful in controlling the acute infection, but the response is slow and has no effect on recurrence. We suspected systemic Candida albicans involvement, but this patient showed none of the characteristic patterns which we rely on for diagnosis of this syndrome.[5] She was, however, particularly aldehyde sensitive. Supplementing her with only 300 micrograms (mcg) of molybdenum has been successful in improving her condition. Controlling the tissue irritation by giving the body the means to handle the excess aldehyde production, this patient's tissue resistance will not be compromised by the infection. She will be able to return to normal tissue resistance following infection and be able to ward off further infections.

The patients with aldehyde sensitivity have complained of many symptoms. Some of these symptoms seem to be directly related to the aldehydes and others from different sources. It is difficult to differentiate which symptoms are aldehyde related in most patients, but the most dramatic responses from controlling aldehyde sensitivity have been in Candida albicans patients, on whom everything else had been tried. The addition of molybdenum, based on aldehyde olfactory sensitivity muscle testing has resulted in turnarounds in our most difficult Candida albicans patients. The most noticeable changes are seen in the sore, achy, sluggish, "flu-type" symptoms of which many Candida patients complain. The energy returns, the generalized musculoskeletal achiness improves, and mental sluggishness disappear, and sinus and nasal congestion clears up. Based on these observations on difficult patients, we now screen every Candida albicans patient with the aldehyde sniffing test and take appropriate measures sooner rather than later in these patients. The addition of molybdenum, in particular, has been a great boon to us in handling the Candida patient, and getting them out of whatever rut or vicious cycle the aldehyde sensitivity has put them into. Molybdenum is also important in caring for a number of other metabolic problems associated with the Candida patient, as well as other patients.

127

MOLYBDENUM AND AMMONIA METABOLISM

Mowles' study included olfactory challenging with ammonia in addition to formaldehyde.[4] There are many facets to olfactory challenging with ammonia which have been discussed by this author in his seminars and are the source of future papers.[7] Mowles chose to focus his study on the relationship of ammonia weakening response to the strengthening response from molybdenum. In twelve patient trials where the patient weakened on sniffing ammonia, seven of these patients were found to have weak muscles strengthen with insalivation of molybdenum.

Molybdenum is necessary for the function of xanthine oxidase enzyme. Iron is also necessary for the function of this enzyme. Xanthine oxidase converts hypoxanthine into xanthine and then converts xanthine on into uric acid. (See Figure 3.) These reactions are essential in the metabolism of purines. It follows then, that patients with low serum uric acid levels should be checked for a need for molybdenum (and/or iron).

$$\text{PURINES} \rightarrow \underset{\substack{\text{XANTHINE} \\ \text{OXIDASE}}}{\overset{\text{Fe, Mo}}{\text{HYPOXANTHINE} \rightarrow}} \underset{\substack{\text{XANTHINE} \\ \text{OXIDASE}}}{\overset{\text{Fe, Mo}}{\text{XANTHINE} \rightarrow}} \text{URIC ACID}$$

Figure 3

Uric acid is excreted in the urine and is one way in which the body may rid itself of ammonia. In Figure 4, one can see that each molecule of uric acid contains four nitrogen molecules. Since the body can synthesize purines from amino acids, carbon dioxide, ammonia, and formate, a lack of xanthine oxidase function could presumably cause a back up in the metabolism of purines and block one pathway of utilization of ammonia. The ammonia from amino acids which would otherwise be used in the synthesis of purines may be backed up in the system. This would explain the observation that sniffing ammonia causes a weakening of some of these patients' muscles. In a number of patients weakening upon sniffing ammonia, the weakening will be neutralized by the insalivation of molybdenum, presumably due to its relationship to xanthine oxidase. (Occasionally iron will also neutralize the ammonia weakening effect, and there are many other factors which must be considered in this olfactory ammonia challenge.)

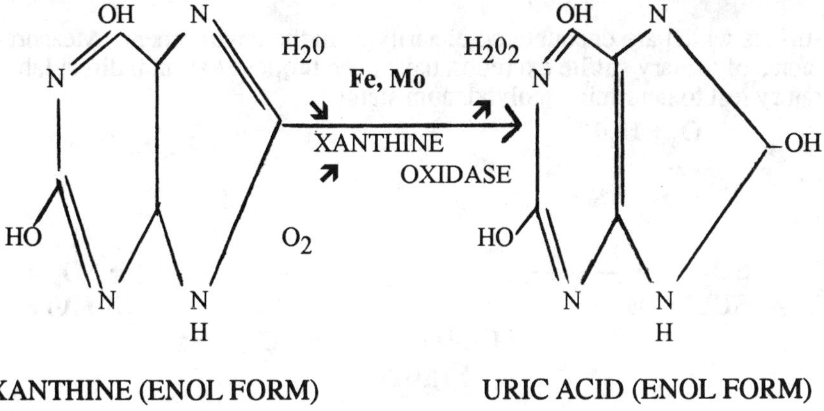
OH
N
N
HO
N
N
H
H_2O
Fe, Mo
XANTHINE
OXIDASE
O_2
H_2O_2
OH
N
N
OH
HO
N
N
H
XANTHINE (ENOL FORM)
URIC ACID (ENOL FORM)

Figure 4

Because there are so many factors related to the ammonia olfactory challenge, it is convenient in ammonia sensitive patients to use a muscle which is weak in the clear for screening for the appropriate nutrients(s). If molybdenum strengthens the muscle which is weak in the clear, it is held in the mouth while the ammonia is sniffed. Supplementation of molybdenum (or any other substance) is based on the nutrient first strengthening a weak muscles, and then negating the weakening effect previously induced by sniffing ammonia.

Ammonia sensitivity is related to many symptoms. The syndrome of hyperammonemia has been discussed by Pangborn[8] and Philpott[9] and others. At least part of the concern with excess ammonia availability in the body is the amination of many substances which have neurotransmitter potential: for example, glutamic acid, when aminated becomes glutamine. Both substances have very different effects in the central nervous system. Likewise, in light of extra available ammonia, histadine will tend to be converted into histamine, aspartic acid will tend towards conversion into asparagine, and the availability of other amino acid putative neurotransmitter substances such as glycine may be affected. Molybdenum deficiency may thereby have some pretty far-reaching effects in the metabolism of purines, ammonia metabolism, neurotransmitter activity, and possibly many other related pathways.

MOLYBDENUM AND SULFITE METABOLISM

Molybdenum is necessary for the function of the enzyme sulfite oxidase. This enzyme plays the important role in the conversion of potentially harmful sulfites to the harmless and useful sulfates in the body. (See Figure 5.) Sulfite oxidase is necessary for the eventual metabolism of sulfur groups in the sulfur amino acid metabolism which begins with the essential amino acid, methionine. This enzyme is also important in dealing with sulfites which are encountered dietarily or in the environment. Measurements of urinary sulfite excretion have been proposed as an indirect laboratory test to determine molybdenum status.[10]

$$O_2 + H_2O \qquad\qquad\qquad H_2O_2$$

$$\searrow \qquad\qquad\qquad \nearrow$$

$$Mo$$

$$SO_3= \rightarrow \text{---} \rightarrow SO_4=$$

SULFITE   SULFATE

SULFITE OXIDASE

Figure 5

Sulfites are used by the food industry as preservatives. Metabisulfite is used to keep fruits and vegetables looking fresh in grocery stores and restaurant salad bars. This substance has created severe reactions in patients who are sensitive to it, and has even resulted in a few deaths. Asthmatics must be especially wary of this substance since it will trigger an almost immediate severe asthma attack. One of our sulfite-sensitive patients thought he had been poisoned and had such dyspnea that he felt like he was dying, collapsing on a restaurant table following eating of a salad from a salad bar in which sulfite preservative was used. He eventually pulled out of the asthma attack, but now he asks first about the use of sulfites when eating out. Another patient in our practice simply avoids eating out altogether because of the fear of ingesting sulfites. Her reaction is extreme nasal and nasopharyngeal congestion, tachycardia and arrhythmia, and complete exhaustion from sulfite contact. These patients will have weak muscles which respond to molybdenum, although their sensitivity to sulfites may or may not be affected by this supplementation, and avoidance of sulfite contact is usually recommended.

The three pathways for the metabolism of sulfur-containing amino acids, starting with methionine, are summarized in Figure 6. In one pathway for the eventual processing of these sulfur containing amino acids, a sulfite ion is released which must be converted into sulfate, using the molybdenum-dependent sulfite oxidase enzyme. Another pathway is the eventual conversion of cysteine into taurine. Still another pathway, also shown in Figure 6, is the conversion of cysteine into what eventually is pyruvic acid and sulfide ion.

Folic
B-12
Methyl ↑
Group

→ METHIONINE
Mg++ ↓
SAM (S-ADENOSYL-METHIONINE)
↓ ↘ CH_3
SAH (S-ADENOSYL-HOMOCYSTEINE
↓
← HOMOCYSTEINE
B-6 ↓
CYSTATHIONINE
↓

SULFIDE
↗
CYSTINE ↔ CYSTEINE → B MERCAPTOPYRUVIC ACID
↘
PYRUVIC ACID

↓ B-6
CYSTEINE-SULFINIC ACID → B SULFINYLPYRUVIC ACID
↓

↓
HYPOTAURINE   ↙ H_2O
↓
TAURINE

Mo^{6+}
↓ $SO_3 = →$ $SO_4 =$
PYRUVIC ACID   ↗   ↘
$O_2 + H_2O$ H_2O_2

Figure 6

What we have observed clinically does not exactly fit what we would expect to see based on the metabolism pathways in Figure 6. A number of patients will demonstrate dramatic weakening of all their muscles when ingesting methionine which will be negated by the simultaneous insalivation of molybdenum. In other words, it appears that in a molybdenum requirement, the body's ability to metabolize methionine is blocked. this may be seen in amino acid profiles by an elevated methionine.[1] This would make sense in the case of magnesium deficiency as can be seen in Figure 6. But in the case of a need for molybdenum we would also expect to find a weakening from cysteine since the role of molybdenum is played beyond cysteine in the metabolic flow chart. We only occasionally see weakening from cysteine in these patients. We occasionally see strengthening from cysteine or no response from cysteine in these patients, but we are surprised at the infrequency with which we observe cysteine to cause weakness in these patients.

Some of these patients will show a strengthening response to taurine. Taurine has been discussed in an earlier paper by this author in its function as a free radical scavenger for the free radical OCl (hypochlorite ion or hypochlorous acid.)[6] In light of a molybdenum requirement, we have observed some patients who weaken on sniffing Clorox who are taurine responders and who also have this weakening response negated by molybdenum insalivation. Although this does not make sense based on the biochemistry presented, there must be some sort of negative feedback mechanism when sulfite oxidase is unable to metabolize sulfites. This feedback must affect the conversion of methionine, causing it to back up, thereby causing the weakening response to methionine we observe in some patients with a molybdenum requirement.

In a few difficult patients who fall into the "fast oxidizers" or "over-oxidized" category, we find a generalized muscle weakness pattern when we first examine the patient. The use of the antioxidants glutathione in combination with selenium has caused strengthening in a number of these patients who did not respond to water or a multiple vitamin or mineral nutrient as recommended by Goodheart.[11] These patients always have symptoms of free radical pathology and are among the most difficult we see. Because of the nature of cysteine being a part of the tripeptide, glutathione, and because of our occasional observations of patients requiring cysteine for production of taurine for OCl free radical quenching, we attempted to check two of these multiple weakness patients with a combination of molybdenum (in place of glutathione) with selenium. We have seen a combination of these two minerals cause a generalized strengthening effect in two multiple weakness patients. One of these patients also responded to a glutathione-selenium combination and the other one responded only to the molybdenum-selenium combination.

Candida albicans allergy [may be] due to the chronic, long term stimulation of the immune system, free radical release, and antioxidant depletion. Imagine the chemical stress a patient's tissues must be under when constantly exposed to free radicals, sulfites, acetaldehyde, and ammonia, all of which have accumulated in the tissues due to an unmet molybdenum requirement of the patient. Add to this the other factors involved in the Candida patient and it is easy to see why Candida can be difficult to treat, and why molybdenum can be such a great help in treating these patients.

MOLYBDENUM AND IRON METABOLISM

In 1981, this author reported the common observation of iron neutralizing retrograde weakening of patients' muscles.[12] Mowles observed that many retrograde type patients responded to molybdenum either in conjunction with or separately from iron.[4] Molybdenum plays a synergistic role with iron in the body. Clinically we are observing that any time one might use iron, one may also find a need for molybdenum.

132

Molybdenum and iron are related in a number of biological processes other than xanthine oxidase and aldehyde oxidase. In plants, there are iron-molybdenum dependent nitrogenase enzymes, for example, as well as several other areas which Mo and iron work together in important roles.[13] In humans, the highest concentrations of molybdenum are found in the liver, kidney (where xanthine oxidase is present) and the adrenal glands. High concentrations are also found in bone and skeletal muscle although , at present, Mo's functions in these tissues is unknown.[13]

We have found muscle testing indicators for Mo to be the same as for iron. This is especially true when a patient has previously shown an A.K. need for iron and still has the same indicator for iron despite supplementation. These patients usually also respond to Mo. We speculate that, for whatever reason, possibly molybdenum's antagonist role to copper, to be discussed in the next section, Mo enhances many of iron's roles. This might include iron's hematopoietic role and its role in myoglobin in muscles. Perhaps, these are some of Mo's unknown functions in bone and skeletal muscle.

Identifying a need for molybdenum has solved several curious cases of apparent iron deficiency anemia when patients were non-responsive in spite of iron supplementation. We now consider a potential for molybdenum whenever we observe a lowered red blood cell count, lowered hemoglobin, lowered hematocrit, or lowered mean cellular hemoglobin (MCH). We have not seen enough of these patients to prove this relationship, but our anecdotal experience is enough to make us suspect a need for molybdenum any time we suspect or find a need for iron. We have also observed Mo cause a response in the case of aerobic metabolism through myoglobin formation. Molybdenum has occasionally been seen to neutralize these aerobic muscle testing weaknesses in some of our musculoskeletal patients.

Candida albicans is an anaerobic organism and therefore grows more readily in an anaerobic environment. Anything which interferes with the ability of the body to carry oxygen to its tissues may enhance the growth of Candida. Molybdenum's apparent functions paralleling those of iron may aid in producing a higher level of tissue oxygenation and thereby decrease the anaerobic environment in which Candida flourishes.

MOLYBDENUM AND COPPER

Molybdenum and copper are antagonists. Just as iron and molybdenum are synergists, iron and copper are antagonists if they are not in balance with each other, so are molybdenum and copper antagonists. In patients who demonstrate copper toxicity patterns, we have traditionally employed zinc and manganese to chelate the excess copper out of the tissues. Molybdenum is also useful for this purpose. Molybdenum antagonizes copper absorption and in a number of experiments in animals, copper and molybdenum have been shown to be directly antagonistic to each other.

133

Mowles and I have observed an extremely high correlation in our practices of copper toxicity in patients with Candida albicans[5] as well as in women with menstrual and premenstrual disorders from functional hormonal imbalances.[14] It is possible that our geographical location (R.M.-Roanoke, Virginia, and W.S. - Chapel Hill, North Carolina) is responsible for this correlation. However, we find such a consistent pattern of low iron-high copper that we suspect copper's antagonism of iron and the resultant tendency toward an anaerobic environment for the yeast to grow as a major factor in these patients, as previously mentioned. [Editor's note: in the brewing industry, replacing copper vats with another metal resulted in brewer's yeast being unable to grow, or ferment barley-rice into beer.]

Occasionally, we see a patient who has Candida and is low in copper. This seems contradictory to our other findings unless it is remembered that copper plays an essential role in working with iron when they are in balance. As we have observed a need for Mo in some iron non-responsive iron deficiency type anemias, others have reported a similar pattern of copper deficiency. Too much or too little copper can interfere with iron's role in hematopoiesis.

When we identify a copper toxic patient, we look very closely for any indication to give molybdenum. This includes any of the above parameters or simply testing any gamma-2 muscle weakness. Gamma-2 (patient-started) weakness implies systemic chemical imbalances which are monitored by supraspinal (e.g., hypothalamus) levels[15] and seem to be involved in all cases in which we find a need for molybdenum.

SOURCES AND DOSAGES OF MOLYBDENUM

The average adult intake of molybdenum in the U.S. has been variously reported as 350 mcg and between 120 mcg and 140 mcg.[13] When a patient requires molybdenum based on one or more of the parameters mentioned in this paper, it is always our policy to supplement the patient with molybdenum for a period of time. We initially recommend 300 mcg. per day and continue this level for one to two months, depending on the patient's clinical response. We always insist that the patient taste (chew or suck) the supplement to activate the taste bud receptors which have direct input to the hypothalamus. After the first month or two, and when the patient's condition has shown improvement, we decrease the dosage to 200 mcg per day until the patient has taken the supplement for a total of four months.

The length of time to supplement a nutrient can often be based on clinical judgment and symptom response. In the case of molybdenum (and a number of other nutrients, especially those which have a relationship to red blood cells), however, we always maintain supplementation for a period of at least four months. This is based on the suggestion of Dr. George Miroff[15] who recommends that any nutrient which is associated with hematopoiesis be taken for a long enough period of time that each RBC in the body gets its full share. In other words, since the life of a RBC is 120 days, it is necessary to take these nutrients for at least 120 days to ensure that the entire blood supply has had the advantage of this nutrient.

We have observed a number of patients who took molybdenum (or other nutrients which aid in RBC production and/or are taken up by the RBCs only during hematopoiesis) for one or two months and became asymptomatic, only to have the symptoms return one or two months later after stopping the supplement. Starting at 300 mcg and gradually reducing the dosage over four months time period has proven successful in our practice. In some difficult patients, we continue supplementation as long as they are symptomatic at a 100 to 200 mcg level.

It is important to note that in cattle, molybdenum excess has been shown to decrease fetal growth.[1] Although no studies have indicated this in humans, we usually stop molybdenum supplementation in our pregnant patients, just to be on the safe side. If the obvious need for molybdenum returns, we will again supplement this nutrient, but at 100 mcg or less as a precaution. Since there is no recognized standard for Mo need, we must rely on good clinical judgment regarding dosage.

After a period of four months, we stop Mo supplementation if the patient is asymptomatic. We recommend that the patient consume more Mo containing foods, if they are not already doing so. Foods which are high in molybdenum are shown below in order of their molybdenum concentrations.[1]

Grains: Buckwheat, wheat germ, barley oats.

Vegetables: Lima beans, canned beans, soybean meals, lentils, green beans.

Liver and sunflower seeds are also high in molybdenum.

Since adding the diagnostic protocols for Mo in our office, we have found scores of patients who showed a need for this essential trace element. The remarkable response in symptoms in patients with Candida albicans as well as other difficult patients has caused us to check each new patient for this mineral. Molybdenum is beginning to creep its way into multiple nutrient formulae by many companies, but the need for the addition of specific Mo supplementation is still a common finding even in patients on these multiple nutrient supplements. With the growing awareness of Candida albicans and other metabolic disturbances which relate to the molybdenum pathways, it is felt that a significant percentage of your patients may be helped in their recovery by identifying the need for and supplying the essential, but little known trace element, molybdenum.

SUMMARY OF MAJOR CLINICAL INDICATORS FOR MOLYBDENUM

1. Muscles weaken on sniffing an aldehyde (e.g., acetaldehyde, formaldehyde, benzaldehyde, etc.) and insalivation of Mo neutralizes this weakness.

2. Muscles weaken on sniffing Clorox (hypochlorite) and/or tasting methionine and/or cysteine and insalivation of Mo neutralizes this weakness.

3. Muscles weaken or sniffing ammonia and insalivation of Mo neutralizes this weakness.

4. Whenever iron is indicated, Mo might also be indicated, such as in: aerobic testing muscle weakness patterns; retrograde position weakness patterns, low hemoglobin, RBC count, hematocrit, or MCH

5. Whenever copper causes muscle weakness, Mo may be necessary to chelate out excess copper. Also discussed: If strong muscles weaken or weak muscles strengthen on sniffing acetones, this indicates a need for B-1.

References:

1 Pfeiffer, Carl. Newer Information on Essential Trace Elements, presentation at "Health by Choice" conference, Atlanta, 1984. Recorded by Insta Tape, Inc., P.O. Box 1729, Monrovia, CA 91016-5749.

2 Pfeiffer, Carl. *Mental and Elemental Nutrients*. New Canaan, CT: Keats, 1975.

3 Pangborn, Jon B. Functions of Taurine Metabolism, presentation at International Academy of Preventative Medicine conference, Chicago, 1983. Recorded by Insta Tape, Inc., P.O. Box 1729, Monrovia, CA 91016-5729 and Technical Memorandum 5: Taurine, August, 1983.

4 Mowles, Richard. A Clinical Study Investigating the Diagnostic Screening and Application of the Trace Mineral Molybdenum in Applied Kinesiology, I. C. A. K. Collected Papers, Summer, 1985.

5 Mowles, Richard and Schmitt, Walter H., Jr. An Applied Kinesiological Approach to Candida Albicans Allergy, *Digest of Chiropractic Economics*, 28:4, January-February, 1986, p. 133.

6 Schmitt, Walter H., Jr. The Clorox Test. I.C.A.K. Collected Papers, Summer, 1985.

7 Schmitt, Walter H., Jr. Manipulating Body Chemistry Seminar, St. Louis, October, 1985. Tapes available from A.K.S.P., 1926 Overland Drive, Chapel Hill, NC 27514.

8 Pangborn, Jon B. The Amino Acid Biochemistry of Hyperammonemia, International Academy of Preventive Medicine Conference. Las Vegas, fall, 1981. Recorded by Insta Tape, Inc., P.O. Box 1729, Monrovia, CA 91016-5729.

9 Philpott, William H. and Dwight K. Kalita. *Victory Over Diabetes*. New Canaan, CT: Keats, 1983.

10 Sohler, Arthur, Molybdenum, Its Metabolism and Role as a Micronutrient. Academy of Orthomolecular Psychiatry 12th anniversary symposium. New York, 1983.

11 Goodheart, George. Personal communication. Summer, 1983.

12 Schmitt, Walter H., Jr. Retrograde Lymphatic Blockage and the Pectoral Stretch Technique: An Indicator for Iron. I.C.A.K. Collected Papers, Winter , 1981.

13 Rajagopalan, K.V. *Molybdenum in Biochemistry of Essential Ultra trace Elements*, ed. by Earl Frieden. New York: Plenum Press, 1984.

14 Mowles, Richard. A Clinical Investigation of Premenstrual Syndrome and the Correlation with Copper. I.C.A.K. Collected Papers, Summer, 1983.

15 Schmitt, Walter H., Jr. Muscle Testing as Functional Neurology. I.C.A.K. Collected Papers, January, 1986.

16 Miroff, George. director Monroe Medical Research Laboratories. Southfield, N.Y. Personal communication. 1984.

A Selected Reading List

Bell, I.R. *Clinical Ecology. A New Medical Approach to Clinical Illness.* Bolinas: Common Knowledge Press, 1982.

Bliznakov, E.G., M.D., & G.L. Hunt. *The Miracle Nutrient Coenzyme Q10. The Revolutionary Breakthrough That Can Strengthen the Heart, Boost the Immune System & Extend Life Naturally.* New York: Bantam Books, 1987.

Carper, J. *The Food Pharmacy. Dramatic New Evidence That Food is Your Best Medicine.* New York: Bantam Books, 1988.

Chaitow, L, D.O., N.D. *Amino Acids in Therapy. A Guide to the Therapeutic Application of Protein Constituents.* Rochester: Healing Arts Press, 1985.

Crook, W.G., M.D. *The Yeast Connection. A Medical Break-through. If You Ever Feel Sick All Over, This Book Could Change Your Life.* New York: Vintage Books, 1986.

Fifty Simple Things You Can Do to Save the Earth. Berkeley: The Earth Works Group, 1989.

Frazier, C.A. *Coping With Food Allergy.* New York: New York Times Book Company, 1974.

Gerber, R., M.D. *Vibrational Medicine.* Sante Fe: Bear &Company, 1988.

Kloss, Jethro. *Back to Eden.* New York: Lancer Books, 1971.

Kreig, M.B. *Green Medicine. The Search for Plants that Heal.* Chicago: Rand McNally & Company, 1964.

Lesser, M. *Nutrition and Vitamin Therapy.* New York: Grove Press, 1980.

Lynes, B. with J. Crane. *The Cancer Cure That Worked. Fifty Years of Suppression.* Canada: Marcus Books, 1987.

Newbold, H.L. *Mega Nutrients for Your Nerves.* New York: Wyden Books, 1978.

Orton, C. *Eczema. A Complete Guide to All the Remedies—Alternative and Orthodox.* New York: Thorsons Publishing Group, 1986.

Ott, J. N. *Health and Light.* New York: Pocket Books, 1976.

Pearson, D. and S. Shaw. *Life Extension. A Practical Scientific Approach.* New York: Warner Books, 1982.

Pfeiffer, C.C. *Zinc and Other Micro Nutrients.* New York: Keats Publishing Company, 1978.

Truss, C. O., M.D. *The Missing Diagnosis.* Birmingham: The Missing Diagnosis, Inc., 1983.

Walker, Morton, D.P.M. *The Healing Powers of Garlic. Nature's Ancient Medicine in Modern Deodorized Form.* New York: Simon and Schuster, 1980.

Zamm, A.V. *Why Your Home May Endanger Your Health.* New York: Simon and Schuster, 1980.

Health Questionnaire

(Data gathered from this questionnaire will remain confidential and anonymous unless you specify otherwise. The intent is to compare populations of people who stay healthy with those who have had Post Polio Syndrome or other Chronic Illness. Out of it may come helpful information to those with problems. The idea is to find out what works for you.)

1. If you had polio, when was the acute stage of infection? _____
Your age now?_____

2. If you had any bulbar or muscle complications, for example, paralysis, was the paralysis visible? For example, atrophied limb, walked with a limp, used wheelchair? Please specify _____

_____

3. Have you been clinically diagnosed as having a chronic illness?_____

4. If so, what are your symptoms? _____

_____

5. If you have not had a chronic illness diagnosed or have not experienced typical symptoms of chronic pain, weakness, insomnia, depression, water retention, speaking difficulties, problems in concentration or memory, chronic fatigue, what have you done to stay healthy? _____

_____

_____

6. Do you take vitamins? Please specify _____

_____

7. Do you take mineral supplements? Specify _____

_____

8. Is your diet rich in fruit, vegetables, and legumes (beans, peas, soy products)?_____

9. How many hours do you work a week?_____

10. Do you pace yourself, take breaks, rests, naps?_____

11. Is chiropractic a part of your routine health maintanence?_____If so, specify how often (1 X year, never)_____

12. Is massage a part of your health program?_____

13. What childhood diseases have you had? (Chickenpox, oral thrush, flu, colds.... please add dates in parentheses e.g. mumps (about 1950)

_____

14. How often have you been given broadspectrum antibiotics (penicillin, tetracycline, etc.)_____

15. Did the recent use of antibiotics precede your chronic symptoms?_____

16. Have you ever been diagnosed for Candida infections?(oral white patches on mouth or gums, fungal infections of nails, lungs, skin, gut, vaginal yeast infections)_____

17. What did you do to take care of it? _____

_____

18. Do you live in a sunny dry climate year round; in a damp, cold moldy climate? Please specify where_____

19. Have you noticed that you experience some problems during some seasons, and few problems during others? Explain _____

_____

_____

20. Do you have gum disease?_____

21. Do you have toothdecay?_____

22. Do you have silver fillings? How many?_____

23. Do you smoke, drink alcohol, crave sweets?_____

24. Do you have a chronic bad temper?_____

25. Are your hands and feet normally warm or cold?_____

26. Do you experience manual or other dexterity problems when the temperature is at or below 68 degrees F.?_____

27. Would you say you were clumsy?_____

28. Do you have problems getting to sleep, or staying asleep unconnected with urinary urgency?_____

29. What vaccines have you taken?_____

30. Have you experienced periodic dizziness?_____

31. Do you have food allergies or other allergies?_____

32. Can you tolerate the smells of cologne, perfume, household cleansers, etc?_____

33. Have you ever experienced metallic, salty, or bad odor tastes on your tongue that you couldn't account for?_____

34. Do you experience gas, bloating, episodes of diarrhea, constipation, hemorrhoids, or heartburn?_____How frequently? _____

35. Have you experienced acne or rosacea as an older adult?_____

36. Do you have dry hands, feet, or hair?_____

37. Do you have eczema?_____

38. Do you take or have you taken progesterone/estrogen, cortisone, steroidal drugs, chemotherapy?_____

39. Do you experience gas or growling in the gut when you eat mushrooms, yeast breads, vinegars, wine, beer, aged cheeses or sugar?
_____

40. Does your salt intake have an aluminum desiccant listed on the label? Grated cheeses? Do you use antiperspirants with aluminum additives?
_____

41. What kinds of diets, therapies, medications, herbs, activity levels do you find helpful in staying healthy? In alleviating chronic symptoms?_____
_____
_____

41. Do you live in a loving supportive home environment? Please describe how your closest family members respond to you.
_____
_____

42. Do you have a positive supportive work environment? Please describe the good news and the bad. _____
_____
_____

43. Would you describe yourself as self confident? Please offer a few details?_____
_____

44. Would you describe yourself as an intense, overachieving Type-A personality or something else? _____
_____
_____
_____

45. Were you an overachiever before your chronic condition, or after, or would you describe yourself as a take-it-as-it-comes relaxed personality?_____

46. How much undisturbed sleep do you get at night?_____

47. Do you feel that you are worthy enough to be well?_____

48. Do you expect to be well? Do you feel, in other words, you deserve to have a full and happy life?_____

49. Do you feel cheated for having had an illnes ?_____

50. What have you learned from being ill?_____

_____

51. Were you excluded from any activity because of illness?_____

52. Describe your physical activity levels. (Yard work, walking, exercise, sports, washing dishes, sitting...)_____

_____

53. Do you feel that you have had to prove something to yourself and the world?_____

54. Would you say you have nothing to prove to yourself or anyone else?_____

55. Have you generally been healthy or have you been subject to many illnesses, or other chronic conditions?_____

_____

56. Please add any information that your observations and intuitions tell you are important, not necessarily what you believe a doctor would want to hear, but what you think positively or negatively affects your health.

_____

_____

_____

Thank you for taking your time to fill this out.

Please return a copy of this questionaire to:

Stephan Cooter
c/o ProMotion Publishing
10387 Friars Road, Suite 231
San Diego, CA 92120

Index

143

copper 24, 67, 76, 99-101, 109, 118, 123-124, 133-134, 136
corn sugar (AKA sugar, corn syrup, dextrose) ix, 120
cramps, calcium for 15; 19, 71, 121
Crawford 81
Crohn's disease 30, 38
Crook 23, 41, 74-75, 88, 91-92, 96, 114
Culbert v-vi
cysteine 115, 130-132, 136

D
Dalakas 9, 10-11, 17, 31, 38
dendrites 49
depression i, 1-2, 6, 16, 20, 23, 25, 38, 48, 50, 53, 57, 58-59,
      71, 76, 82, 90, 104, 113, 117, 120
detoxification ii, 10; & glutamine 45-46; 50;
      & molybdenum 98; 118
dexterity 1, 24-25
dextrose ix, 120
DL-phenylalanine (DLPA), pain & depression 58-59;
      deficiency symptoms 60
dopamine 53, 55, 60
DPT shots vii-viii, 5, 7, 35-36
drunk-disease 39
Duesberg vi
dysfunction & hypothalamus 5, 7, 43;
      & neurotransmitters 55-57; & ATP 64; 75-76, 84, 99
E
eczema 26, 43, 40, 45, 53, 75, 120-121
Eldepryl 9, 53; compared with DLPA 60
Ely 51
Eng i, 50
environment 2, 35, 41-44, 51, 53, 73-74;
      & mold 76; 78; love 83-84; 88, 91, 93-94, 104-105,
      107, 124, 126, 130, 133-134
Epstein-Barr 2, 113

F
fatigue i, ii, x, 3, 6-7, 29, 32, 34-35, 40, 50, 53-54,
      58-59, 63, 65, 68, 85, 97-98, 113, 115, 117, 120-121
fatty acids 34, 63, 67, 90
Fibromyalgia (FM) v, 6, 53, 120
fluorescent lights 44
folic acid 102, 115-116, 120-121
food allergies 2, 51
food supplements 3, 45, 107
formaldehyde vi, 43-44, 102, 118-119, 125, 128, 136
free radicals 50, 67, 118, 132

fresh juicing 63
Friedman xi-xii

G
GABA 60
garlic 92-93, 96-97, 104, 106
Gerber 82, 83, 85, 87
germanium 50, 109
ginseng 48-50, 63, 67; & detoxification 50
glutamine 1; & detox, addiction 45-46; 115, 119-121, 129
gold 100, 109
grades & illness 89
gum disease 40-41, 65-68, 107

H
hangovers & aldehydes 39
(Mad) Hatter's syndrome 43
Hermes, Trismegistus, the outside & the inside 89
herpes x, 6-7, 29-34, 114
HHV-6 vi
holistic 15-16
hydrogenated 73, 75, 95, 101, 106, 115
hyperventilation (Type A, alkalosis, & mineral loss) xii
hypothalamus lesions ix;
        & Type A rats xii; 7, 20, 22, 24-25, 47, 55, 60, 97, 119, 134

I
illness, purposes of 86, 91, 94
inositol 57, 60
insalivation 126, 128, 131-132, 136
insomnia i-ii, v, 1, 3, 10, 21-22, 25-26, 38, 40, 48, 50;
       & niacin 60; 85, 90, 113, 117, 120

J
Japan 7, 39, 50, 63, 65, 69, 96, 106, 108, 109

K
Kloss & mineral deficiency theory of illness 26, 50, 57-58, 64, 99
KM (herbal potassium supplement) 15, 20-21
Krebs cycle (citric acid cycle) 64

L
language 84-85
Lazzarini 11
lead ii, xi, 24, 40, 44, 72, 78, 101, 120
Leung 50
love 80, 84, 88
lupus ii, vi, 3, 6, 12, 30, 38, 65, 84, 90, 93, 109, 113

lysine xiii, 29; virus, concentration, weight loss 33-35; deficiency symptoms 34; 92, 93

M

Magic Johnson 5, 12, 111

magnesium 16; deficiency symptoms 22-24; 71, 73, 71-78, 99-100, 115, 121, 131

Malmstrom 51

manganese 16, 23, 63-65, 67, 76, 99, 115, 121, 133

massage xiii, 15-20, 46-48, 54, 57, 69-70, 78, 83, 91, 110

Maynard 43

measles xi

memory x, xii, 1, 8, 38-39, 51-52, 55-56, 57, 59, 76, 113, 117, 119

meningitis v, viii-xi, 5-6, 31, 35, 87

mercury vi, 7, 12, 24, 43-45, 50-52, 76-77, 83, 99, 118, 121

metabolism 7, 23, 25, 32-35, 45, 64, 67, 75, 93, 99, 100-101, 105-124, 125-126, 128, 129-133, 136

metallic taste & candida 41-42

methionine 115, 129-132, 136

Miller, JR 11

minerals xi, 24; herbalist's theory of illness 26; 54, 67, 76, 88, 91, 97, 99-100, 109-110, 114-115, 121, 132, 136; mineral wasters (coffee, soft drinks) 23

molybdenum ii, xii-xiii, 6, 95, 97-109, 113-118, 120-136; & ammonia 118-121, 128-129; & sulfites 118, 124, 129-130, 132; & aldehydes 98-100, 124, 126, 132, 136

multiple sclerosis (MS) ii, v-vii, xi, 6, 9, 30, 37, 43, 51, 53, 63, 90, 95, 100-102, 109, 118-120, 122

mumps x

Murray vi, 22, 35, 103, 116, 122

N

natural foods 26, 45, 107

nerve(s) vi, x, 2, 9-10, 16, 21-22, 24, 29-32, 38, 43, 55-58, 63-64, 69-72, 75-76, 99, 101, 116, 119

Nerve Tonic 63, 69-72

nervous system 2, 15-17, 20, 25-26, 30, 39-40, 47, 49-50, 54, 56-57, 64, 90, 114, 116, 121, 129

neurotoxin 8, 12

niacin (B3) 1, 60, 115, 124-126

nizoral 92, 106

nutrition 8, ii, 3, 5, 11, 16-18, 22-23, 36-37, 46, 55, 57, 61, 69, 83, 90, 109, 123

nystatin 37, 75, 92, 73, 93, 95-98, 106, 113, 127

O

oregano, oil of, & candida 96-97, 101, 106

Ornstein xii

over-achieving 6; motives behind 80; 88-89

P

Sabin vaccine 5, 6, 10-12
Salk vaccine 5, 10-11
salt xii, 21, 69-71
saponins 50
Schmitt 1, ii, xiii, 97-98, 100, 116, 118, 122-123, 136
Schrieber 46
Schuessler 70
Schwyzer 102
selenium 1, 63, 65, 67, 76, 100, 109, 115, 121, 132
Selye 47
Shaw 55, 57, 59-60
shingles 7, 29, 31-34, 71
SIDS (sudden infant death syndrome) vi-viii
Simian virus vi
soma 20, 85
Sood vii
sudden remission 51
sugar (AKA refined carbohydrate, dextrose, corn sugar,
        fructose, fruit sugar) 1, v, ix-xii, 16, 23, 41, 45-46,
        57, 77-78, 90, 95, 102, 106, 114, 116, 119-122
sulfites 118, 124, 129-130, 132

T
T-cells 31, 66
taurine 60, 115, 118, 130-132, 136
Taylor, Allen ii, 18, 78
Taylor, Joyal 51-52
Tepley 80, 84
thyme & lemon 54
thymus 56, 82
tricyclic antidepressant 1-2
Truss 37-41, 96, 114-115
tryptophan 60, 120; in food for sleep 60
twitches (muscular, AKA fasciculations)
        & calcium 15; & magnesium 22; & mercury 52
Tylenol 20, 57
Type A behavior & illness xi-xii, 6-9, 20-21, 87-91, 94;
        & acupuncture theory 60-61; & lack of self worth 73, 84, 85

V
vaccination campaigns vii
vaccines ii-xii, 5, 7, 10-12, 35-36, 53, 87-88, 110
vegetable oils 65, 75, 114
virus vi-x, 2, 5-12, 20-22, 29-33, 35-36, 38-39, 46, 66,
        81, 87, 89, 92, 93, 104-106, 113
vitamin A 44, 46, 67

149

vitamin B1 (thiamine) v, ix; & nail polish remover 125, 136
vitamin B12 116
vitamin B3 (Niacin) & sleep, 60; & aldehydes 115, 124-125
vitamin C 23, 45-46, 76
vitamin D 16; & nervous system 24-25; 116
vitamin E 50, 63, 65

W
Waksman 11
water 2, 6, 13, 24, 41, 45-46, 65, 71, 76, 121, 132
weakness i-ii, v-vi, x, xii, 1, 3, 5, 21, 29, 32, 38, 54, 56,
         58, 64, 65, 81, 85, 89-90, 97-99, 113, 117, 132-134, 136
weather 5, 13, 16, 20, 24-25, 30, 41, 57-58, 70, 73
weight control mechanism 29, 34
weight loss 29
white bread v, x-xi
white flour 1, xii, 33
white rice 1, v, ix-xii
whooping cough (see pertussis) 7, 35-36
Wiley ix, 110
willow bark & Peruvian Bark (7-R),
         compared to other pain killers 18-19
worthiness 82-84
Wyckoff 92

Z
Zheng Gu Shui 48
zinc & colds 35; 67, 76, 92-93, 99, 121, 133